Sex Linkage of Intelligence

Recent Titles in
Human Evolution, Behavior, and Intelligence

Sex Linkage of Intelligence

—— *The X-Factor* ——

ROBERT LEHRKE

Human Evolution, Behavior, and Intelligence
Seymour W. Itzkoff, Series Editor

 PRAEGER

Westport, Connecticut
London

Library of Congress Cataloging-in-Publication Data

Lehrke, Robert Gordon.
    Sex linkage of intelligence : the X-factor / Robert Lehrke.
        p.   cm.—(Human evolution, behavior, and intelligence, ISSN
    1063–2158)
    Includes bibliographical references and index.
    ISBN 0–275–95903–1 (alk. paper)
    1. Intellect—Genetic aspects.   2. Genetic psychology.   3. X
chromosome.   I. Title.   II. Series.
BF431.L4328   1997
155.7—dc21   96–53612

British Library Cataloguing in Publication Data is available.

Library of Congress Catalog Card Number: 96–53612
ISBN: 0–275–95903–1
ISSN: 1063–2158

First published in 1997

Praeger Publishers, 88 Post Road West, Westport, CT 06881
An imprint of Greenwood Publishing Group, Inc.

Printed in the United States of America

The paper used in this book complies with the
Permanent Paper Standard issued by the National
Information Standards Organization (Z39.48–1984).

10 9 8 7 6 5 4 3 2 1

Contents

vi   Contents

Illustrations

Figures

Tables

Preface

A hundred thousand or so years ago when human beings first learned to put ideas into words, they also started trying to find the answers to a lot of questions. At first those questions related to the events in their own lives. "Why are there so few berries where there used to be lots of them?" "Where are the animals when I want to kill them for food?" "Where does the sun go at night?" "Why did my favorite mate die?"

To answer these questions, they made up theories. The natural forces at work were beyond their understanding, but they could see that people could cause things to happen and so they attributed that same power to plants, animals, and even inanimate objects. So they decided that the berries had become angry because someone had done something wrong in their presence; the animals had decided to go on a trip elsewhere to spite them; the sun, like a burrowing animal, had gone under the ground. When it came to personal misfortunes, perhaps those happened because an enemy caused them to. That is, when a favorite mate died, it may have been because of the spell cast by an envious neighbor. If too many bad things happened, it might be best to do away with that neighbor.

That kind of thinking still exists in the world. In fact, at least until recently, the bushmen of Australia felt that they were perfectly justified in doing away with a neighbor if they were satisfied in their own minds that the neighbor was the cause of their problems. And not too long ago, in our own part of the world, the "witches" of Salem were tortured and killed in the belief that they were the cause of problems in the community.

However, even in a very primitive society, the idea of blaming personal enemies for misfortunes was counterproductive. If one killed one's neighbor, on the assumption that he (or she) was the cause of one's problems, the neighbor's kin were probably aware of the cause of *their* problems. Whereupon, the situation was ripe for still another killing.

Thus such personalization of the source of one's misfortunes lost favor, although it never quite disappeared. That kind of thinking still exists, even in the so-called civilized world, although now the blame isn't necessarily placed on a single individual. Nowadays, the blame for many misfortunes is placed, not on natural events, but on Congress, the administration, the school board, the police, the courts, the Democrats, the Republicans, the Communists, the system. It is much simpler to blame SOMEBODY than to try to understand the complex events involved in the misfortunes of the world. The idea of retribution to the presumed source of the problems also still exists, although only in a few instances does it involve actual killing. For instance, normally we just vote the rascals out of office.

Later on in prehistory, a little more elaborate type of theory evolved. It wasn't one's malevolent neighbor who caused the creek to dry up. There was a new invention: gods. These gods, who could be human or even animal in form, controlled the sun and the rain and the migrations of the animals, not to mention events in everyday life. If a god was angry, one had better do something to appease him or her. Such deification has not disappeared. The pastor in the little rural church in Minnesota I once attended still prays for rain or, at haying time, for the rain to stop. And some of the parishioners really believe that these prayers have been answered when the rain, in due time, does start or stop. They operate on the theory that their god does indeed exert direct control of the forces of nature.

Now, to an increasing extent, the more sophisticated among us look for an understanding of the forces of nature, including human nature. When it comes to the physical sciences, we have reached remarkable levels of comprehension and, to a lesser extent, of control. This has been a gradual process. First, early scientists observed and studied objects or phenomena. Then the more creative among them tried to find an order in their observations, to develop a *theory* that tied them together.

When an apple fell from the tree in the vicinity of Isaac Newton, he didn't decide that the gods were angry at him and were trying to hurt him, nor even that they were pleased with him and trying to present him with a treat. (After all, the apple was probably rotten, or it wouldn't have fallen.) What he did was to develop a *theory*, the theory of gravitation, to explain what happened. The nature of this theory was such that it could generate testable *hypotheses*. Upon extensive evaluation of such hypotheses by means of experiments and measurements, which consistently confirmed the theory, it became a scientific law, the law of gravity. Without the findings made possible by the theoretical approach, many of the miracles of modern science would be impossible.

When Charles Darwin and Alfred Russel Wallace proposed a theory to account for their separate observations about the origin of species, it was much more difficult to come up with definitive experimental proofs, although repeated observations of natural phenomena have validated their findings to an extent acceptable to all but a few. However, even as a theory, their ideas are much more useful, in a scientific sense, than the magical or mystical theories espoused by the creationists, which do not lend themselves readily to any but a very simple sort of a logical system.

In this book two theories are presented. One, going back to my doctoral dissertation in 1968, is that the genes controlling the growth pattern of major intellectual traits are located on the X-chromosome. This may now be more than just a theory. Recent research into the cause of the single most common cause of mental subnormality, now generally called the fragile-X syndrome, has provided evidence that seems to confirm the X-linkage of major intellectual traits at the molecular (chromosomal) level.

A secondary theory is that higher human intelligence arose out of a mutation, or series of related mutations, on the X-chromosome. This theory, like the evolutionary theory of Darwin and Wallace, will probably remain a theory indefinitely. However, it fits known data, including some recent molecular findings, so precisely that it probably will eventually be accepted as the best available approximation of the truth.

The theory of X-linkage of major intellectual traits has over the years been written up in my books and professional papers, which are listed in the Table of References in the back of this book. This has exposed the ideas therein to the judgment of professionals, who have in turn written hundreds of learned papers in books and professional journals on the subject. However, the book you are now reading is the first general publication of the theory relating to the evolution of higher mental processes. That, too, is now a sitting duck for the learned professors and researchers to examine and criticize.

However, this book is not written primarily for such people. To the best of my ability, I have tried to discuss the theories and their implications in a manner that is understandable to reasonably bright people in general, and to give a little of the scientific background of the evidence. It is such people—the leaders and professionals in the community, not the learned professors—who are more likely to use the ideas immediately to help solve many of the problems faced by our society today.

And now for the traditional "thank you's". While there is a certain amount of "first person" narrative in the book to follow, especially in reference to the origin of the theories involved, a book such as this one does not arise out of the work of a single mind. Over and over in the text I have given credit to my mentor, John Opitz, M.D., who introduced me to the subject of X-linkage and who guided my early research. Behind the scenes in the writing of this book there was a friend and former student, Dave Cary,

Ph.D., who read every word, sometimes several times, and whose comments and editorial assistance have been invaluable. As a specialist in the areas of race and gender, his insights have helped me to avoid offending with ill-stated ideas or poorly chosen words in these sensitive areas. He has also been a great help in searching out reference materials.

It would have been much more difficult to do write the final version of this work had it not been for my computer, introduced to me—nay, imposed upon me—by my youngest son, Allen, who continues to answer my sometimes stupid questions about how the darn thing works. (It has reached a point in our civilization that the old must learn from the young). Then there is my daughter, Patricia, and my other son, Bob, Jr., plus my late wife, Mary, all of whom did without a lot of things so that I could continue my education long after most men are well established in their careers.

This book met with many rejections before Dr. Seymour Itzkoff honored me by including it in his *Human Evolution, Behavior, and Intelligence* series so that it could be published. And last but not least, my thanks go to Dr. James Sabin and the staff at the Greenwood Publishing Group for their cooperation in getting the book into print. This applies especially to Mr. Matt Christianson whose patience must have been sorely tried as he guided me through the intricacies of turning out camera-ready copy.

Sex Linkage of Intelligence

Chapter 1

Background

In the first [phase of human history], five races of an extinct form of man, Homo erectus, inhabited the land surfaces of the Old World south of the winter frost line, except in China where one race dwelt north of it. By the time phase one began, these men had already learned to make recognizable tools and probably to speak, and before long some of them had learned to keep warm with fire and to cook food. By the middle of this phase at least one race of Homo erectus had evolved into a race of our present species, and before it was over Homo erectus had vanished from the earth. This was essentially a biological phase of history, in which the possession of a superior capacity for culture gave Homo sapiens a decisive immediate advantage, and an opportunity for the future.

Carleton S. Coon

In his book, *The Story of Man*, Coon (1962a) expanded on a theory first set forth by Weidenreich (1946) that Man (as *Homo erectus*) was already divided into five primary races when *Homo sapiens* came on the scene. *Homo erectus* then disappeared from the scene by evolving into something else, namely, *Homo sapiens*. This was later expanded in another book, *The Origin of Races* (Coon, 1962b). In his last book, *Racial Adaptations*, published posthumously in 1982, Coon surmised that the appropriate threshold from *Homo erectus* was crossed by each race, "either by its own mutations or by impregnation of its women by *Homo sapiens* invaders" (p.139).

While earlier theories concerning Man's origins went so far as to suggest that the existing races were descended separately from altogether different simian species (whites from chimpanzees, blacks arising from gorillas and mongoloids from orangutans), Weidenreich (1946) and later Coon modified that to the view that primitive Man's ancestry went back to different lines of fossil Men, for instance, Peking Man being ancestral to modern mongoloids and Rhodesian Man to the sub-Saharan Africans (Swartz and Jordan, 1976).

A more modern view is that the term "race" simply refers to a population that has bred in relative isolation for many generations and has acquired evolved characteristics that can be distinguished on the basis of genetically determined physical traits. While such genetically-determined characteristics as skin and hair color cannot be determined directly from the skulls and bones of ancient finds such as "Lucy" (Edey and Johanson, 1989), and only to a limited extent can intelligence be inferred, there are characteristics that *can* be measured from skeletal material. For instance, there are notable genetic differences between such diverse populations as the Nilotic tribes of Africa and the Eskimos of North America and northern Asia, which differences are presumed to be related to climatic conditions. In tropical Africa, tall, slender people would have a greater skin surface area relative to body mass, allowing greater dispersion of heat and would therefore be more likely to survive and reproduce. Short and stocky Eskimos would have proportionately less heat loss and therefore an evolutionary advantage in a cold climate (Weiss and Mann, 1985).

The contrary, and prevailing, view when Coon's work was gaining a great deal of public attention, was that *Homo sapiens* was a new species, as different from those that had previously existed "as horses, zebras, and donkeys" (Coon, 1962a, p. 28). This suggested that interbreeding with *Homo erectus* was impossible, or at least unlikely. The progenitor of this new subspecies was generally interpreted as being Cro-Magnon Man. The other genera and species of Man simply disappeared.

However, since Cro-Magnon Man was a fairly recent species, going back only 30,000 or 35,000 years, a lot of questions were asked. In particular, how could the different races have evolved separately in that relatively short period of time? The rather acrimonious debate that resulted will be summarized briefly in chapter 5.

Then, in 1987, Cann, Stoneking, and Wilson at the University of California in Berkeley came up with an entirely new date for the origins of modern Man. Using the mutation rate of mitochondrial DNA as a yardstick, and a complex computer program, they calculated that humans of all races are descended from one female ancestor who lived 200,000 years ago, more or less. That effectively eliminated Cro-Magnon Man as the common ancestor of modern-day Man. This was confirmed after Allison Brooks and John Yellen discovered in Africa some highly sophisticated tools that antedated Cro-Magnon Man by about 100,000 years (Perlman, 1995). In addition, Dr. Richard L. K. Fullagar of the Australian Museum in Sydney and his colleagues (cited in Bower, 1996b) have described artistic renderings in Australia with an estimated age of 58,000 to 75,000 years, suggesting that the modern type of Man had spread that far, long before Cro-Magnon Man appeared.

One other question remained. What was there about the genes of this "Eve", the 10,000th grandmother of us all, that led to the selective survival of her descendants? There must have been well over a million of the species *Homo* inhabiting the earth at that time (Dobzhansky, 1962). Was it really greatly enhanced intelligence, "the superior capacity for culture," as Coon (1962a, p.9, quoted above) suggested? If so, how did it arise?

The answer proposed in the following chapters certainly fits. It also answers a lot of other puzzling questions related to present-day problems. For instance, why are there so many more males than females with mental subnormality, learning disorders, and inability to learn and adapt to the behavioral norms of society; while at the same time there is good evidence, not only from history and current events but from psychological test data, that there are more males who are exceptionally bright, or who are highly talented in a variety of fields?

And why does hereditary sex-linked mental deficiency (now often called the fragile-X syndrome), which is by far the most common form of mental subnormality, apparently fail to conform to one of the axioms of population genetics, namely the Hardy-Weinberg Law? That is, why does the number of cases of sex-linked mental subnormality tend to remain stable or increase in the population, when (as a genetic lethal) it should be gradually disappearing (Opitz, 1986)? This is both a scientific and practical problem of great importance.

Why do racial or ethnic groups, on an average, differ so markedly in the nature of their special talents, such as cognitive ability and athletic skills? (Even more important, perhaps, is what can, or should, be done to compensate for these differences, or perhaps to take advantage of them in a positive sense?)

For each of these questions many answers, or explanatory theories, have been or could be devised. However, according to the laws of logic, a single theory that provides answers to all of them, and to many other questions of like nature, would be preferable to a lot of piecemeal answers. The following pages provide just such a single answer. It probably is less than perfect as it stands, but it does provide a starting point for a fresh look at Man's greatest asset, human intelligence, and it leads to a few suggestions regarding solutions for some of the problems our society faces today.

One precaution. It must be made clear that the "Adam" story discussed in chapter 2 and the early chapters of this book is an *allegory* which is based on a theory derived from conditions and phenomena reported or observed in the present-day world. That is to say, the "Adam" theory of the origin of higher human intelligence arose out of the theory of X-linkage (sex linkage) of higher human intelligence, which is the primary subject of this book, not vice versa. It did not originate from archeological data, although it is largely confirmed by such data; and while archeological and anthropological terms and concepts have been used in this book in discussing the evolutionary basis for the mutations that are the basis of modern human intelligence, this is mainly a matter of linguistic convenience. In the literature there are already terms, such as *Homo erectus* and *Homo sapiens*, that can be redefined to fit the theory.

In addition, an attempt has been made to fit the "Adam" story into what is already known (or surmised) about Man's origins. No substantial contradictions have been found between existing *knowledge* and the new theory, in spite of the fact that the new ideas disagree with current conceptions about the origins of *Homo sapiens* in many ways.

To summarize, the early chapters of this book will propose a theory of how higher human intelligence arose as a consequence of mutations on the X-chromosome. The later chapters will discuss what is far more important today, the consequences of such X-linkage.

Chapter 2

The Big Leap

> The Mutant Molecular disease is closely connected with evolution. The appearance of the concept of good and evil that was interpreted by Man as his painful expulsion from Paradise probably was a molecular disease that turned out to be evolution.
>
> Linus Pauling, Nobel Laureate

Adam

We'll call him Adam, because that was the name he was given by those who recorded myths and legends about a quarter of a million years later. And Adam did, in a figurative sense, "eat of the fruit of the tree of knowledge of good and evil" as the Bible says. He was the first creature to have the capability of foreseeing the more remote consequences (for good or evil) of his actions, or even of having a comprehension of such concepts as "good" and "evil". That was, in the eyes of those who originated the Biblical story of Man's beginnings, the most important way in which he differed from the animals.

Adam was a mutant. As the result of an alteration in the regulatory genes on his X-chromosome, actually nothing more than a change in the number of molecules between a structural and a controlling gene, the growth pattern of certain neuronal connections within his brain was altered so that his intelligence continued to increase, not for the 5 years or so typical of his parents and contemporaries, but for 15 or more years. Such neotenous (youth-prolonging) mutations (which are discussed in more detail in chapter 6) can result in dramatic evolutionary changes in a single generation (Montagu, 1962).

Most of the time such changes in the genes would have been neutral in effect, or even harmful—one of the molecular diseases mentioned by Dr. Pauling (1963) in the quotation at the beginning of the chapter. We know now that many genetic alterations such as Huntington's disease (Ross and Folstein, 1993), spinocerebellar ataxia, and many other genetic disorders (Travis, 1995) are due to similar changes in genetic material.

In Adam's case, as it occasionally happens, the change was beneficial since it led to greater ability to adapt and survive. Moreover, we now may assume from recent evidence (Travis, 1995), that remutations at this site may cause partial or even full reversion to the primitive levels.

Whether Adam was a happier creature with his increased understanding isn't clear. The writer of the Book of Genesis assumed that he wasn't; and more recently the English poet, Thomas Gray, in his *Ode on a Distant Prospect of Eton College,* agreed:

> Thought would destroy their paradise.
> Where ignorance is bliss,
> 'Tis folly to be wise.

In any case, the longer period of growth of neuronal interconnections that resulted from Adam's mutation led to a far greater complexity of the part of the brain related to cognitive and language functions. It probably had little effect on his ability to learn by rote or experience, nor on his capability for remembering past experiences and knowledge. These abilities had long since been established in the evolution of the species *Homo.* In effect, the new mutation increased Adam's logic, not his lore. It did give him far greater ability to plan ahead effectively, to solve problems without actual trial and error, to think in conceptual terms, and to use language far more complex than the simple system of signals that existed in his time.

So by this rare chance, the most intelligent creature that had ever inhabited the earth came into being—just another baby boy born somewhere in the Old World (but probably in Africa) about 200,000 or 250,000 years ago. His parents, given modern clothes and haircuts, could probably walk down the street in their part of the world today and not be noticeably different from anyone else. Probably their heads would be a bit small or oddly shaped by today's norms, but not to an obvious extent.

The mutation in Adam didn't result in any great physical changes as far as we can tell now. For the first year of his life, his growth, both physical and mental, was probably much like that of any other baby of that or the present time. Thereafter, although Adam did not differ from neighboring children in bodily growth, the connections in his brain increased much more rapidly, and so did his mentality. By the time he was five, he knew all of the simple words and signs used by his mother and the males who, for varying lengths of time, shared food and bedding area. He was a most unusual little boy, but it wasn't likely that the dull creatures around him noticed that.

His intellectual abilities continued to increase until he had passed about 15 summers; and he learned, very quickly indeed, from his mother and the older males, how to survive in a world that was far from being a Garden of Eden. He could gather food—nuts, berries, fruits, seeds, eggs, even insects and grubs. There were many sources of meat, including some rather large animals, although he usually did better scavenging the kills of the predatory animals than by hunting for himself. In fact, Adam probably learned from others how to use fire, not only for warmth but also for the purpose of tenderizing meat so that his all-purpose teeth could chew it. Long before he was physically mature, his cleverness made him an important member of the group.

Because he was exceptionally capable at bringing home the main course, he became a favorite with the women who, being hampered with babies or children at their side, couldn't go afield in search of food as readily as the males. Many was the night he slept beside such a woman, learning from her the delightful games men and women play together. He probably returned with fair regularity to a particular mate or, later in life, to a few mates; but if his hunting had led him far afield, he was usually not hard pressed to find a woman to share the food he had obtained and his body warmth. He managed to stay alive longer than most, living by his wits long after his physical strength started to fail, and all during these years he was unknowingly starting many babies. Neither Adam nor his mates made any connection between their fun and games and the subsequent arrival of the infants.

Adam's Children

Although Adam's children usually had some degree of physical resemblance to their father, they didn't share his level of intelligence. The boys, of course, didn't inherit the mutant X-chromosome from their father, receiving his Y-chromosome instead. While the girls did, its effect was probably greatly diminished or even canceled out by the old-style X-chromosome they inherited from their mothers.

In fact, it wasn't until Adam was an old, old man, nearing his forties, that a few boys, some of his daughters' sons, showed the same high level of intelligence as their grandfather, having received the mutated gene from their mothers. Still later, some of the bright grandsons mated with their cousins or half cousins, or even their sisters, and of these matings came a few girls who were as bright as their fathers, having received the mutant X-chromosome from each parent.

Since sex was mainly a reward for the bringing of food and a mutually pleasing game, the bright and dull people for a long time mingled and mated freely. However, the bright males were much more successful in getting regular mates as well as in keeping themselves, their mates, and their offspring well fed and safe. In Darwinian terms, they had an advantage in both sexual and natural selection. The bright women could be choosy too, and so more and more of their matings were with the bright men. When this happened, all of the children, both boys and girls, had only the new type of X-chromosome and so were of the new subspecies that we now call *Homo sapiens*. These bright people used their wits to take over the choice shelters and the best food-gathering areas, forcing the duller ones out into the hills where food and shelter were scarcer so that they gradually died out in that vicinity.

New Colonies

Even so, the descendants of Adam eventually reached a population level where many of them had to move on to other valleys. Here, again, many of them mated with the aboriginal population, combining their genetic characteristics. Occasionally the aborigines were of a different genetic (racial) stock; and in these cases, after a hundred generations or so, the physical traits of the original and invading groups had combined, creating a new ethnic type. However, all of those that survived carried the genes for increased intelligence, which was necessary for existence in what had become a more sophisticated world.

After hundreds of generations, then, the bright people—*Homo sapiens*—were well established in that part of the world. They gathered in small groups, probably comprising the female descendants of one or two women, plus their children and their current mates. They kept in touch with other groups in their vicinity for sociability, as a source of mates, and for cooperation in the hunt. It had reached a point where the vegetable foods they gathered, the leftovers from the hunting animals' meals, and the fish and small animals they could capture, didn't provide enough food for everyone. In order to capture the larger or swifter animals it was better to have a large group of males and unencumbered women.

But in such communities there was always a chance for conflict, not only over hunting rights and the distribution of the game, but also over the favors of the women, whose services were needed for a full life. As a consequence, it would not be surprising if, from time to time, a few males would be driven from their group to wander far from their ancestral valley to a substantially different part of the world. They had no trouble in keeping alive as they wandered for months and even years.

So it came to pass that one such group eventually reached another populated area, far removed from its own. It was a pleasant river valley in what is now southern Europe; the game was plentiful, and there were caves for shelter. Most important, there were women—women, oh so stupid and vulnerable, but unusual and beautiful, with fairer skin than they had ever seen. The native men, too, were stupid and easily outwitted, so the intruding men simply took over their caves, their mates, and their daughters for additional mates. And in time there were the bright grandsons and the bright great-granddaughters. Once more the descendants of Adam had taken over a part of the world and spread their intelligence to another race.

The Elimination of the Aboriginals

Not only did the new people monopolize the supply of food and game, keeping it from the aboriginal population, but in time the aborigines themselves may have become fair game. These apes, who looked like people but certainly weren't, couldn't run any faster than Adam's descendants. Although they might pick up stones for weapons, or flail away with a stick of wood or a bone, or even a bone dagger, they were no match for men with such modern weapons as flint-tipped spears and with far greater cunning.

So it would not be surprising if they became an occasional part of the diet of the elite population. Archeological evidence in the form of skulls and long bones cracked open by means of tools indicate that something of the sort must have happened. The flesh and organs of the victims could have been easily whacked off with a sharp stone knife and cooked or eaten raw on the spot or carried in chunks to a convenient place, but the soft, tender contents of the skull took some effort to remove. Therefore the hunter would bring the entire head back to his cave, where he could crack open the base of the skull and extract the brain at his leisure.

Delicious! But that is why, hundreds of centuries later, paleontologists had the nerve to say that primitive man was cannibalistic. It is possible that sometimes he did eat one of his fellows, but that, in the opinion of Montagu (1969), was probably for magical or religious purposes. For instance, he might eat a particularly feared foe that he had overcome in order to magically take on his strength and cunning.

But when he devoured the muscles and organs or cracked open the skulls and long bones of the arms and legs of individuals of the *Homo* species simply for food, it probably wasn't his own relatives that he ate. While the supply lasted, he may have occasionally hunted and eaten those foolish wild men who didn't have enough intelligence to make good weapons, or to talk much, or to escape the wiles and traps of the real people of the valley. It was all right to throw their skulls into the corner of the cave when the edible parts were gone. As to his own kin and friends, when they died or were killed, the remains were ceremoniously buried, or at least they were removed from the living area to a remote spot where the wild animals could dispose of the remains.

For those who don't like the idea that their ancestors were cannibals, there is an alternative explanation that also fits the data. The earlier specimens of *Homo*, and even some more recent ones, probably weren't the bold hunters of legend but scavengers who would gladly settle for the remains of kills by predatory animals (Johanson and Johanson, 1994). Suppose the carcass in a particular instance was that of an individual of the species *Homo*. By the time the original predator, the scavenger animals such as hyenas and jackals, and the carrion-eating birds got through with a carcass, it is probable that all that remained were large bones, too heavy for the scavengers to break, and the skull, too large and heavy to be crushed even by a lion, a wolf, or a bear. With or without a knowledge of the original source of the bones, a hungry *Homo* might well be glad to latch on to these remains, realizing that by means of such tools as a flint hand-axe he would be able to extract the edible contents for himself and his hungry family.

A Continuing Process

The story of the spread of the new type of Man was repeated over and over. Sometimes the descendants of Adam extended their living areas, gradually mixing with, and providing their superior brains to, the aboriginal population. (It should be noted that these aboriginals, *Homo erectus*, were technically of the same species as the new type of Man, *Homo sapiens*, since interbreeding was possible).

In other cases a few wanderers invaded, and their descendants took over, additional lands. In the former case, the physical traits of the intruders blended with those of the original population, so that the descendants were a combination of both types. In the latter case, the physical traits of the intruders were soon covered up by those of the far greater numbers of the aborigines, leaving as a relic of the descendants of Adam only the trait of higher intelligence, which had become essential for survival.

Thus the descendants of Adam spread throughout the world, displacing and finally eliminating those other specimens of *Homo* that weren't bright enough to compete. Intelligence and invention made it possible for them to survive even in areas of the world where part of the year was cold, since they could plan ahead to provide food, fuel, and shelter during the winters. It is possible, indeed likely, that in the colder, less hospitable regions there was greater need for, and therefore greater selection for, higher levels of intelligence than in the warmer climes.

The question may arise as to why Man migrated into these cold regions, away from the hospitable warm climates where he originated. It certainly wasn't intentional. However, a group would move from an existing settlement to a less crowded area where there was less competition for food and shelter. Such a move might have been no more than a few miles, not far enough to make a noticeable difference in climate. However, over thousands of generations the accumulated distance led them north (or less frequently south) to colder areas of the world. As they reached the colder areas of the world, even into North America, their survival rate was reduced, but the population growth continued, though at a far slower rate.

In any case, *Homo erectus* had become *Homo sapiens*. He was now "wise man".

Cro-Magnon Man

Perhaps 150,000 years later another mutation arose in southern Europe that may have resulted in a further increase in the intelligence of those who carried it. This one led to a greater proliferation of the basic brain cells; and the resulting larger brain resulted in a larger skull, because the growth of the skull is determined almost entirely by the size of its contents. Like the "Adam" mutation it was probably neotenous, resulting in the prolongation of the growth pattern of entire brain cells (not just the nerve fibers, as in Adam's case) for longer than the 5 months after conception that is still characteristic of humans. In other words, while individuals of the original species of *Homo*, like modern Man, had all of their brain cells by 5 months gestational age, this mutation probably resulted in a longer period of multiplication for such cells.

However, mutations are not correlated from one organ system to another (Dobzhansky, 1970). The mutation for larger head size, with some of the additional growth occurring before birth, was not accompanied by corresponding enlargement of the female pelvis, resulting in difficulty in passing the infants through the birth canal.

For a while, selection took care of the matter. Only veritable Amazons survived giving birth to one of these big-headed infants, and they tended to pass on to their offspring of both sexes their genes for excellent physique as well as those for larger brains. Even so, over time the discrepancy between skull size and the capacity of the birth canal eventually led to the elimination of the Cro-Magnon subspecies which Graham (1989, p. 130) has described as "the most magnificent creatures Nature has ever produced". The bearers of just the original "Adam" mutation did not, of course, suffer the same fate, since much of their increase in cranial size occurred after the child was born, as it still does.

The Basis for the Story of Adam

The story of Adam and his descendants is, of course, allegorical, but there is strong evidence that it is basically true. Much of the factual material can be found in the remarkable book, *The Origin of Races*, by Dr. Carleton Coon (1962b). This, along with other works, has been interpreted in light of a theory of X-linkage of major intellectual traits first put forth by the author in his doctoral dissertation in 1968 and subsequently in other publications listed in the bibliography at the end of this volume.

It should be apparent that the story does not pretend to cover the entire process of the evolution of Man from his simian ancestors. It does not, for instance, relate to such other human adaptations as the opposable thumb, upright position of ambulation, teeth and digestive system adapted to a wide variety of foods, and the development of tongue, lips, and throat suited to the production of the complex sounds used in speech. Important as these other changes were, it was the advanced development of the brain—the ability to learn from verbal as well as environmental cues, to plan ahead, and to solve problems without actual trial and error—that has led to Man's domination of the world.

There is a brief and decidedly readable summary of the wider range of human evolution in Dr. Ashley Montagu's (1962) book, *Culture and the Evolution of Man*. Interestingly enough, Dr. Montagu points out that many of Man's other major mutations were, like the one relating to the growth of neural connections within the brain, neotenous. This can account for the relatively rapid evolution of the species *Homo*.

An example is Man's angle of gaze which, unlike that of most four-legged animals, is at right angles to the spinal cord. This condition is noted only in the early fetal stage of four-legged animals such as dogs and cats, but it persists through pre- and post-natal development in Man and certain simians.

It should be evident that what is inherited is not some predetermined final outcome, but a *pattern of growth*. Barring accident or disease, this growth pattern results in a certain range of outcomes.

The Origins of Human Variation in Intelligence

It may appear from the foregoing that the X-chromosome Adam inherited from his mother remained the same through generation after generation. The truth is that it didn't. For one thing, the growth-controlling element was superimposed upon an already variable set of genes. For another, the process of crossing over of chromosomes during meiosis (the formation of new egg and sperm cells) resulted in constant changes within the mutated area. This was exaggerated in the earlier days by differences between the primitive and mutant forms of the critical area of the X-chromosome. It is not unlikely that within a few scores of generations after Adam the variability in human intelligence, or more specifically in cognitive ability, was almost as great as it is now.

The Right-Brain Mutation

Somewhere along the line, and somewhere in the world, but most likely in what we now call Europe, a second mutation occurred. This mutation, which probably evolved as a secondary consequence of the slight aneuploidy (unbalanced chromosomes) resulting from the "Adam" mutation, affected the other half of the brain to a greater extent. Some of this part of the cortex probably originally related, as it presumably still does, to Man's ability to orient himself in space—to avoid getting lost. One of the results of the new mutation was to give the males in possession of it, and females who had it on both X-chromosomes, greater ability at perceiving other types of spatial relationships—of seeing how things went together, so to speak. This type of ability was identified as X-linked by Stafford (1961). This second mutation wasn't quite as important in an evolutionary sense as that related to verbal and conceptual ability, and it didn't spread nearly as rapidly. Even today it seems to show up in its more favorable forms on only about half of the X-chromosomes in the U.S. population (Bock and Kolakowski, 1973).

Nonetheless, the possessors of that mutant section on the X-chromosome have probably been responsible for much of the industrial revolution, since it would lead to mechanical inventions, enhance certain aspects of engineering ability, and increase the number of persons with the ability to assemble and repair mechanical devices. It is also possible that there have been other mutations at that site. Among the possibilities are those related to advanced mathematical ability and exceptional musical creativity. These may, of course, be variations of either the original mutation or of the one related to other kinds of spatial perception, but the evidence that can be derived from the *idiot savant* phenomenon (discussed later in this book) is that the genes involved are separate from those for cognitive ability. At least there is clinical evidence that they have a different developmental schedule, which suggests that they have separate genetic controls.

Hypotheses: The Implications of the Adam Story

The story of Adam and his descendants, brought up to the present, provides the basis for a dozen relatively simple hypotheses. Note, however, that the basic theory of X-linkage of major intellectual traits does not stand or fall on the basis of any one hypothesis.

1. A significant mutation related to the growth or development of the parts of the brain involved with cognitive and language ability occurred on the X-chromosome of an individual of the species *Homo erectus*.

2. The mutation was probably due to a change in the number of nucleotides (a fairly common evolutionary event) in a small area of an egg-producing cell of a woman who lived about 200,000 years ago. By particularly fortunate chance, the site of the mutation was on the X-chromosome rather than on one of the autosomes, with the result that the consequent phenotypic changes would be expressed immediately in any male to receive the mutant chromosome. It would not, however, be fully expressed in a female unless she had inherited the mutant gene from both parents.

3. By nature, the mutation was neotenous. That is, its effect was to maintain a youthful characteristic, that of continued growth of certain connections within the brain, for an extended period, by comparison with that of others of the species *Homo* alive at the time.

4. Being an aneuploid, or unbalanced, type of chromosomal event, the new mutation was unstable, since it resulted in erratic pairing of homologous chromosomes during meiosis (the formation of chromosomal complements during the creation of new egg or sperm cells). Because it was unstable, further variations of the original mutation occurred, resulting in considerable variation in the new genes and in their phenotypic expression. These variations were undoubtedly subject to evolutionary selection.

5. The part of the brain most affected by the primary mutation was that portion of the temporal region related to cognitive and language functions. The basic centers for these traits were, of course, already present in a primitive form, but the mutation caused their neural interconnections to develop for a longer period of time and thus to a far greater complexity.

6. These new abilities resulted in a tremendous evolutionary advantage, both in terms of natural selection and sexual selection. That is, not only were the individuals who expressed the gene(s) better able to survive long enough to reproduce, they also had an advantage in obtaining mates and in keeping them and their offspring alive. Consequently, in spite of a possible slight and temporary decrease in basic fertility, due to the small mismatch of the X-chromosomes with those of the aboriginal population, the carriers of the new genes increased in relative numbers.

7. From its start in a single individual (or possibly two or more brothers), the mutant type of *Homo* spread within its original group, replacing the older type within a relatively few generations. Then, in groups and as individuals, persons carrying the new genes infiltrated other areas occupied by the older type of Man. When mixtures involving large groups occurred, racial characteristics (which were already well established) became thoroughly intermixed. When just a few individuals introduced the new genes to a population, the racial characteristics of the aboriginals remained, submerging the variable genetic characteristics of the invaders except for the improved intellect.

8. Because, as previously mentioned, the new mutation was unstable, further mutations at the same chromosomal location have occurred, affecting somewhat different traits. One of the most obvious and important of these paralogous genes relates to the development of the non-dominant half of the brain. While the characteristics of the so-called "right brain" are not yet well defined, they do include control of the organs of speech for the production of language. It is likely that another function is related to the ability to deal with geographical space, that is, to get around without getting lost. The mutated gene may also have increased the ability to perceive spatial relationships on a smaller scale, including what might be called mechanical ability. Other changes may include mathematical and musical abilities and probably others not clearly defined. It is possible that this mutation actually occurred first in human evolution but did not become especially meaningful until the "Adam" mutation made it so.

9. Being relatively recent in evolutionary terms, the chromosomal area of the mutation has not yet become stabilized. This instability can result in occasional fresh mutations. Some of these mutations can be expected to result in mental deficits or disabilities which, being sex-linked, are more frequently manifested in males. The most damaging of such harmful re-mutations would probably result in the type of X-linked mental subnormality commonly called by such eponyms as Renpenning's syndrome or the Martin-Bell syndrome, which may actually be a partial or complete throwback to *Homo erectus*, modern Man's final evolutionary ancestor. In fact, continuing instability at this new (in an evolutionary sense) chromosomal locus may well be an explanation of the so-called fragile-X phenomenon that is almost invariably associated with mental subnormality, autism, or other mental disorders.

10. The hypothesis that the effects of the X-linked genes, normal or abnormal, show up in the growth patterns of certain areas of the brain can be used to explain many previously puzzling aspects of mental retardation and

learning disorders. In cases where an allele (variant) of the X-linked genes results in a relatively slower onset or development of the neuronal connections involved in cognitive development and/or spatial perception, there could be difficulty for the affected individual in adapting to the rigid, age-specific demands of school and society—mental *retardation* in a literal sense. When the delay involves only a limited area, the condition is more likely to be considered a learning disorder. In at least a few cases, such a slower start could be offset by a longer or more rapid period of growth before leveling off. That pattern, which would be more often apparent in males, could explain many cases of school failure in persons who, as adults, turn out to be in the normal range of intelligence—normal but under-educated. *In effect, due to X-linkage there would be expected to be greater male variability in the age of readiness for basic education.* Furthermore, if it should be the case that such slower maturation is more frequent among children of certain ethnic groups (both boys and girls would be affected), that could be of great significance in planning educational programs for them.

11. Because a boy receives his only X-chromosome from his mother, the adage, "Like father, like son," does not apply to cognitive and to other X-linked abilities to the same extent as to traits related to autosomal genes.

12. Even more significant, X-linkage can be expected to lead to greater male variability in those areas of intellect that are X-linked. The greater number of males at the highest levels of accomplishment, then, is not a matter of chauvinism and sexual politics. Neither is the greater prevalence of mental subnormality and learning disorders among males primarily a social and behavioral phenomenon.

Each of the above hypotheses will be discussed in more detail, starting with chapter 4. While the collection of data supporting each hypothesis is far from encyclopedic, enough is presented to justify the assumptions made and to provide a basis for further research.

The Author's Apologies

The author recognizes that many persons of both sexes will disagree with the Adam story and the theory of X-linkage of major intellectual traits. Many may even find the X-linkage theory, many of the hypotheses related to it, and especially its implications, distasteful or even offensive. However, no matter how strongly one believes in one's philosophical predilections, that does not give them scientific validity. Therefore, if, on the basis of one's personal philosophy, one puts the whole idea of X-linkage of major intellectual traits out of mind, one may be putting aside the basis for an understanding that will help solve many of the problems people are facing today.

Others will point out that there are possible alternative explanations for each point of supporting data. However, in that case they would be ignoring the logical principle of *parsimony,* often called "Occam's razor". That is, a single explanation that fits *all* of the data is more acceptable than a lot of explanations each covering only a part.

Perhaps the theory and its correlates are deeply disturbing, or even threatening, to people who have long held different opinions. But, if a person who has always considered himself or herself to be a picture of health, on hearing a physician say, "That spot on your lung is possibly cancerous," finds the idea unbelievable or threatening and therefore refuses to take action in the matter, he or she risks harming mainly himself or herself and those close to him or her.

However, if scientists and persons of responsibility refuse to face up to the possibility of genetic differences in intelligence, whether between individuals, groups, or sexes, on the basis that it isn't "nice" or "politically correct" to think that way, they are taking a serious risk of passing up the opportunity to understand the basis for many problems faced by educators, social scientists, legislators, administrators, the judiciary, and even school children today. Through such understanding they can work to correct those problems.

Philosophy vs. Science

In effect, it is all right, even necessary, to have certain philosophies and customs on which to base personal decisions, since there simply isn't enough time in a life span to consider all of the implications of one's every act. However, when making major decisions, especially those affecting other people, ideally one must go beyond personal philosophy and evaluate matters objectively, scientifically, and in light of all available knowledge of how such decisions affect the larger community, not just oneself and one's own little sphere. Knowledge, or science, as opposed to personal philosophy, should be the criterion. Would that our leaders had the wisdom to understand this.

Will Durant, in the preface to the second edition of his acclaimed book, *The Story of Philosophy* (1943, p. 2), makes clear the relationship between philosophy and science in the matter of decision making: "But is philosophy stagnant? Science seems always to advance, while philosophy seems always to lose ground. Yet this is only because philosophy accepts the hard and hazardous task of dealing with problems *not yet open to the methods of science.*" [Emphasis mine.] The implication is that as soon as there is enough knowledge available to allow decisions to be made on a scientific basis, philosophy can and should give way to reason.

The risks of clinging to a philosophy in the face of knowledge are only too well borne out by recent events in Russia. Communism would seem to be a beautiful philosophy, carrying to the ultimate the idea that, in a moral sense, all Men are created equal. The problem is that such equality is a moral or philosophical concept, not a scientific fact. For instance, it does not mean that all people have the same capabilities or the same motivation. As a consequence, communism just didn't work as a basis for a large governmental system. To make matters worse, even in the face of continued failure the leadership would not back down from its philosophical underpinnings, nor from trying to fit the country's social, economic, and even scientific systems into their interpretation of the philosophical framework. Finally, the system just broke down.

Chapter 3

In Other Words

In 1984, a group of priceless fossils was put on display at the American Museum of Natural History in New York (Begley and Carey, 1984). They were used to illustrate a basic calendar of what was assumed to be Man's ancestry. The consensus at that time was that the hominids in the direct line of modern Man's descent were:

Sivapithecus - 17 million years ago;
Australopithecus Afarensis - 5 million years ago;
Australopithecus Africanus - 3 million years ago;
Homo habilis - 2 million years ago;
Homo erectus - 1 million years ago;
Homo sapiens (Cro-Magnon Man) - 35,000 years ago.

Several others, including *Australopithecus robustus*, were considered to be off-shoots whose lines simply died out.

These bony remains did indeed show a pattern of progressively larger skulls, culminating in Cro-Magnon Man. There was also a progression of increasingly sophisticated artifacts associated with some of the fossils. However, there was still a conflict. Modern Man (*Homo sapiens*) was presumed to have originated with Cro-Magnon Man. Certainly the skull size was suitable. In fact, the Cro-Magnon skulls were often much larger than those of modern Man. In addition, the tools and other artifacts were far advanced; and in the same general area where the remains were found were remarkable examples of cave art.

There were, however, a few questions, including those going back to Dr. Carleton Coon's (1962b) book, *The Origin of Races*. Under the most widely accepted version of Man's ancestry, it was assumed that during the

35,000-year interval between Cro-Magnon Man's appearance and the present, two things had happened. *Homo sapiens* had not only migrated from southern Europe to all parts of the world, eliminating in the process the more primitive forms of *Homo*, but had developed into five major races with numerous subraces. Dr. Coon not only cast doubt on the assumption that the races could have developed in such a short time, but he provided substantial evidence that racial characteristics were already present in some of the more primitive stages of the species *Homo*. This finding was all the more remarkable because at the time Dr. Leakey's discovery of *Homo Habilis*, the immediate predecessor of *Homo erectus*, had not yet been reported.

Logically it does seem doubtful that a 30,000-year interval between Cro-Magnon Man and the dawn of history allowed enough time for the noted racial differentiation. Neither, one would think, did it allow time for the development and differentiation of the world's languages.

Still, only a few scientists accepted Coon's hypothesis. As Volpe (1981, p. 216) put it, "Nevertheless, we do not believe that the Cro-Magnons originated simultaneously in widely different parts of the world. Rather, the Cro-Magnons arose in one place, then migrated to various regions of the globe and became differentiated into geographical races".

In addition, there was a certain amount of disagreement as to the date of origin of *Homo sapiens*. Kurtén (1972, p. 127) pointed out that:

> We do have some evidence of a greater age for typical Homo sapiens than the 30,000-40,000 years ago when the great takeover took place. First, the 40,000-year-old boy or girl from Great Niah Cave is definitely as old as some Neanderthalers and southern Homo erectus or older. Then there are the finds from the Kanjera deposits in Kenya, discovered by Leakey in 1932. They consist of four skulls and a thighbone, all of them quite modern in type except that the thigh bone is rather thick.

He goes on to describe even older fossils that fit the pattern of modern Man rather than the primitive types and summarizes with, "So we cannot get around the fact that *Homo sapiens*, at least in an early guise, was present in Europe in the Eemian interglacial period, most probably in its earlier part, about 100,000 years ago".

Further evidence of both the time and place of the origins of *Homo sapiens* continues to pop up. For instance, to quote David Perlman (1995) of the *San Francisco Chronicle*:

> An extraordinary trove of carved bone tools discovered on the banks of an ancient river is leading scientists to conclude that sophisticated tool-making behavior must have emerged in Africa, not Europe, and many thousands of years earlier than once thought.

Perlman was referring to the discoveries of archeologist Allison S. Brooks and her husband, John E. Yellen, at three sites along the Semiki River in Zaire. Here they found bone harpoon tips and spear heads that reflected a great deal of ingenuity, dating back to the Middle Stone Age, which lasted from 130,000 to 30,000 years ago. While radio-carbon dating was inappropriate for determining the age of the bone tools, there were other, newer methods that showed them to be at least 80,000 or 100,000 years old. In effect, there is increasing evidence that *Homo sapiens* was in existence many millennia before Cro-Magnon Man put in his appearance.

The Argument Goes On

Both sides of the argument had logical weaknesses. Those with the traditional view, that *Homo sapiens* arose from Cro-Magnon Man, would have been hard put to explain a pattern and rate of evolution that would make possible the differentiation of the races in only a few thousand years. On the other hand, Coon (for good reasons, as it turned out) could not integrate his findings with the most generally accepted calendar of human development. For instance, how could the individuals of five major races have separately developed along such remarkably similar lines? As Volpe (1981, p. 217) said,

> It is, however, exceedingly difficult to imagine how several hominid races, diverging in different parts of the world, can evolve independently and yet repeatedly in the same direction leading to only one species, Homo sapiens. . . . Indeed modern evolutionists are disposed to relegate the Weidenreich-Coon notion of parallel evolution of races to the category of the highly improbable.

It should be noted that at this time the impression seems to have been that language and cognitive abilities were within the capability of the pre-*Homo sapiens* types (Pilbeam, 1970) and that most of the development of language and intellectual skills arose out of increased learning along with an almost Lamarckian evolution of the brain centers. In fact, a great deal of attention was paid to the possible development of the organs of speech, as if that were a major limitation keeping Man from developing speech and language (Pfeiffer, 1972; Bower, 1989).

In effect, the traditionalists seemed to agree with Darwin's (1871, Ch. 3) idea regarding the final stages of Man's evolution:

> The mental powers in some early progenitor of man must have been more highly developed than in any existing ape, before even the most imperfect form of speech could have come into use; but we may confidently believe

that the continued use and advancement of this power would have reacted on the mind itself, by enabling and encouraging it to carry on long trains of thought. A complex train of thought can no more be carried on without the aid of words, whether spoken or silent, than a long calculation without the use of figures or algebra.

Notice again the Lamarckian idea of the basis for evolutionary change. This is understandable, since a widespread knowledge of Mendel's ideas about genetic transmission of traits was still a half-century in the future at the time of Darwin's book, while Lamarck's work had been published about 50 years previously.

Furthermore, there was a lapse of many years before Mendelian genetics were incorporated into the Darwin-Wallace theory of evolution. In addition, the idea that *Homo erectus* was congenitally incapable of higher level language and logic does not seem to have occurred to them.

Of Mitochondria and Men

The most serious blow to the traditional (Cro-Magnon origin of *Homo sapiens*) theories about the later stages of Man's origins came from the findings of Cann, Stoneking, and Wilson (1987), which moved the date of the origin of *Homo sapiens* back a couple of hundred thousand years. With that information, the pieces are starting to fall into place, at least as far as the later stages of human evolution are concerned. For one thing, the original *Homo sapiens* could not have been Cro-Magnon Man, who came on the scene much later.

The first reports of the Cann-Stoneking-Wilson findings appeared in the press, for example the Associated Press (1986), but the formal presentation came on New Year's Day of the next year (Cann, Stoneking and Wilson, 1987) with the appearance of an article in the journal, *Nature*. What the authors demonstrated was a high level of probability that all living humans have as a common ancestor a woman who lived roughly 200,000 years ago. They also suggested that the origins of *Homo sapiens* were in Africa.

A few questions did arise regarding the Cann, Stoneking and Wilson (1987) data. Although the basic type of calculation had been done for years in determining the evolutionary distance between different species, for instance Man and gorilla, the Berkeley group could not arbitrarily choose two races of Man as being the most widely separated in an evolutionary sense. Instead they used a computer program to draw up what they assumed to be the most parsimonious family tree for the races of Man, going back to a common ancestor.

Furthermore, the measure previously used, i.e., the number of mutations that had occurred in the genes for certain proteins such as hemoglobin, was far too coarse for the purpose of such a measurement. However, the researchers used the number of mutations occurring in the mitochondria in every human cell as a basis for measurement. It wasn't until almost 5 years later that their methods of using the computer program were questioned (Begley, 1992). One of the problems was that they used some specimens (placentas) from black women in the United States as representative of the African population. They justified this procedure by the logic that prior to the early or middle 1900's virtually all interracial matings in this country involving blacks had been between black women and non-African men. Consequently, (although one of their number, Dr. Mark Stoneking, had his qualms about the matter), they felt that they were justified in assuming that the mitochondrial line of these subjects remained basically African in origin, since mitochondria are transferred between generations only in the female line (Brown, 1990).

However, the researchers did acquire additional specimens and recheck their figures (Vigilante, Stoneking, Harpending, Hawkes, and Wilson, 1991). The findings of the second study simply confirmed and refined the original. "Eve" must have lived between 166,000 and 249,000 years ago.

These findings were confirmed in general by Dr. Robert L. Dorit of Yale University, who based his conclusions on the relative lack of DNA changes in the Y-chromosome, which is passed on only from father to son. The conclusion of the study, as reported in the May, 1995 issue of *Science*, was that modern Man must have originated no more than 270,000 years ago to have so few differences between the Y-chromosomes of men of different races. As Dr. Dorit said, "There's something tantalizing about the fact that two completely different parts of the genome are beginning to tell the same story." (quoted in Adler, 1995). In effect, the evidence is piling up that modern Man's ancestry goes back not much more than a quarter of a million years, but certainly long before Cro-Magnon Man walked the earth.

Was "Eve" an African?

Many people, for both good and questionable reasons, could not accept the findings regarding the probable African origins of Man. For instance, Dr. Alan R. Templeton had legitimate questions as to the way the computer program was used. He reran the data, correcting the previous deficiencies, and although he came up with only minor questions regarding the time of the origination of modern Man, he did feel that the computer program as used did not indicate *where* that ancestor lived with sufficient certainty, since the statistical level of probability was 92 percent instead of the accepted 95 percent (Templeton, 1992). In his opinion, other sites in the Old World were entirely possible from a statistical point of view.

The original authors did recant *on this aspect*. Unfortunately many people took this to mean that the entire study, including the time factor, was faulty, thus throwing out the baby with the bath water, so to speak.

Hedges, Kumar, Tamura, and Stoneking (1992), also re-computed the Cann, Stoneking and Wilson data, with generally the same results. Their conclusion was that while the evidence of African origins was strong, it did not quite reach statistical significance at the .05 level. In their words: "Although an African origin for humans is supported by other kinds of data and other molecular data, and is suggested by the mtDNA [mitochondrial DNA] sequence data, the available sequence data are insufficient to statistically resolve the geographic origin of human mitochondrial DNA." (p. 739)

Thus, the site of the garden of Eden could have been almost anywhere in the Old World. Nonetheless, the students of skulls and artifacts and, with less assurance, the statisticians, still consider Africa to be the prime choice.

Other evidence supports a tropical or subtropical origin of the species, which might, however, include southern and eastern Asia. The early types of human must, of necessity, have existed in a region where fruit and vegetable foods were available throughout the year because of their constant need for vitamin C. Almost all animals have the genes for a process by which vitamin C, which is essential for life, is synthesized within the body. However, that gene was lost during the evolution of the higher simians, and so wasn't passed on to Man's predecessors. Because vitamin C is not stored in the system, Man and his prehuman antecedents would have needed a year-around source.

Later, as Man moved away from the tropics, this lack would have had serious consequences, such as the deficiency disease, scurvy. It is probable that *Homo sapiens* individuals were able to survive the moves to colder regions of the world because they learned to make wine and beer, and to pickle or otherwise preserve vegetable foods to fill this need during the cold months. How the proponents of the Volstead Act (Prohibition) would have hated the idea that fermented drinks were a key to Man's survival!

Some Interesting Questions

The Cann-Stoneking-Wilson (1987) findings raised some other interesting questions. In particular, what was there about the genes of this primitive woman that was so adaptive that only her descendants are now alive? Perhaps there is another question. How can the mitochondrial genes Cann et al studied be used to demonstrate the existence of what (in spite of the objections of Dr. Wilson, who headed the project) came to be known as the

"African Eve"? For non-biologists there may be still another question. What are mitochondria?

Mitochondria

Actually mitochondria are extremely small organs within each cell of all but the very lowest forms of life, both plant and animal, that provide the energy the cell needs to carry on its functions. The number in a cell depends on the energy requirements of that cell. Each human muscle cell, for instance, requires about 600 mitochondria to keep it supplied with fuel; certain other cells need only half that many (Young, 1989).

A most interesting characteristic of mitochondria is that they are actually independent organisms having their own genetic material even though they exist within nucleated (eukaryotic) cells—in other words, cells containing regular chromosomes. This genetic material is basically a few single strands of DNA loosely attached within the cell membrane of the mitochondrion, similar to that of the simplest one-cell organisms such as bacteria. However, that means that mitochondria reproduce independently of the larger cells in which they exist. They are actually cells within cells.

Furthermore, they are transmitted from generation to generation only in the cytoplasm (non-nuclear material) of the cells. Since spermatozoa and pollen have no cytoplasm, the male stock does not pass on any mitochondria to serve as a starter stock for the next generation, and therefore mitochondria are passed on only in the female line. While males receive mitochondrial "seed stock" from their mothers, they do not pass it along to their offspring.

Another characteristic of mitochondria is that their genes have a rate of mutation 5 to 10 times as great as those on the nuclear chromosomes. The number of differences (due to mutations) in comparable amino acid sequences of proteins has long been used to provide a measure of the evolutionary distance between species, that is, the combined time to a common ancestor. However, that is too coarse a measure for the relatively short interval to the time of Adam. For instance, Nobel laureate Linus Pauling has estimated that there has been one effective mutation in each of the hemoglobin chains about every 14.5 million years (Pauling, 1963). That knowledge can be used, for instance, to estimate the time since Man and chimpanzees arose from a common ancestor, a matter of 10 or 15 million years; but trying to figure the date of the divergence of the subspecies of *Homo sapiens* from a common ancestor by means of the number of chromosomal mutations is like trying to measure the diameter of a hair with a ruler.

However, Cann, Stoneking and Wilson (1987) did use the mutations of mitochondria which provided a better measure of such relatively short times, with a scale more on the order of tens of thousands of years than of millions. As a consequence they could make measurements of the genetic distance between existing racial stocks of Man. Their conclusion was that all humans (i.e., *Homo sapiens*) have as a common ancestor a woman who lived about a quarter of a million years ago.

Why Did Eve's Descendants Survive While Others' Didn't?

But let us return to the question of what it was about the "African Eve" that made it possible for her descendants to continue to survive on earth, and not those of the other half-million or so *Homo erectus* females that existed at the time (Dobzhansky, 1962). The late Dr. Allan C. Wilson, co-leader of the group that did the study, puzzled over that question in a lecture before the American Association for the Advancement of Science (Associated Press, 1989). He did speculate that perhaps it related somehow to the ability to speak, since Dr. Luigi Luca Cavalli-Sforza and colleagues at Stanford University had pointed out that that ability seems to have arisen at about the same time as "Eve" put in her appearance. However, it would take some very convoluted reasoning to explain any connection between cellular biology and language.

Mitochondria and X-Chromosomes

Nevertheless, Dr. Wilson missed the point that Eve's mitochondria were passed along *in parallel with her X-chromosomes.* One of these X-chromosomes could have been the site of a mutation that she passed on to at least one of her children, and which provided such a great evolutionary advantage that its possessors have taken over the world; while those who may have inherited her other X-chromosome simply died off over many generations. In all likelihood, the critical X-linked gene was the one for the capability of higher level cognitive ability and speech.

Actually, it cannot be said that Eve passed on her X-chromosome, in its entirety, to her descendants. Because of chromosomal crossing over, her descendants now have an almost infinite variety of gene combinations on the X-chromosome. However, of her descendants over thousands of generations, those strains of *Homo* that carried the tiny segment that led to increased intelligence were far more able to compete for survival and reproduction at a level that assured the continuation of their genes.

Who Was Right?

It is highly probable that Dr. Coon was correct in stating that the races of Man existed before *Homo* became *sapiens*. What he was unable to explain was how the same genes for language and higher intelligence could have become the norm in each separate race.

As Kurtén (1972, p. 127) put it:

> At this point we are presented with the outlines of a major problem. Almost everywhere, either Neanderthalers or late Homo erectus were replaced more or less suddenly by modern types of Homo sapiens. Moreover, these invaders show different racial traits which must have taken some time to evolve. But where did *Homo sapiens* originate?

This leads right into the "Adam" theory. Such a process is exactly what would have happened when one or a few of Adam's descendants (whatever *their* origins) introduced the critical gene into each racial group. Over time, the genes for the physical characteristics of the intruder(s) would have been covered up by those of the far larger native population, so racial characteristics would have remained the same. However, the genes for language and higher intelligence became necessary for survival and reproduction and eventually became characteristic of the entire population.

Quoting Kurtén (1972, p. 138) again, "*Homo erectus* was intelligent enough to get along very well in his environment. But *Homo sapiens* was even smarter and so he crowded out *Homo erectus*."

Errors of the Traditional Theory of Man's Origins

The supporters of the traditional (Cro-Magnon origins) viewpoint seem to have made two major mistakes. First was the assumption that the brain of *Homo erectus* was capable of supporting complex speech and thought. *Homo erectus* was assumed to have simply learned to be *Homo sapiens*.

The second mistake was the assumption that modern Man's common ancestor was the Cro-Magnon subspecies. Cro-Magnon Man was more likely to have been a mutant form of *Homo sapiens*, derived from the Neanderthal strain, and probably, as Graham (1989) said, the most remarkable example of the species that ever existed. However, he came along far too late in prehistory to be the founder of the species; and although his very large brain may have made him exceptionally bright, it probably also led to his downfall, as the prebirth growth of the infants' heads caused them to become too large to pass safely through the birth canal. This would have been even more of a problem in matings between Cro-Magnon males and females of the original Neanderthal type.

Point Mutations and Evolution

Another problem that limited anthropologists in their understanding of the evolution of higher mental skills was that they had been taught that evolution was solely due to cumulative small mutations, which were acted on by Darwinian selection. Such cumulative point mutations do, indeed, account for much of evolution, not only for humans but for all species of organisms, from the simplest on up. In any type of living organism there are, from time to time, changes in the structural genes (those affecting the composition of proteins). If such changes occur in an egg or sperm (or ovum or pollen) that is involved in a fertilization, the resulting changes can be operated on by Darwinian selection. That is, any resulting changes in the organism's phenotype that are deleterious will reduce the likelihood that the affected organism will survive or reproduce, and the gene change is sooner or later lost to posterity. Those chromosomal alterations that result in no change, or that result in changes that are merely neutral, have no evolutionary effect, although the gene change itself may well continue to show up in the descendants.

Only a relatively few gene alterations result in positive changes. These are not only likely to continue to exist but, due to natural and sexual selection, to increase in relative frequency in the population. They are the basic materials of evolution.

It is well established that most differences between individuals within a species actually are due to such small mutations over a long period of time. When, for some reason such as geographical separation, the total number of differences between groups becomes so great that matings between them do not occur or are sterile, a new species or subspecies has been formed.

For instance, the horse of today is larger than its ancestor of ten million years ago. Its close relative, the donkey, which evolved from that same common ancestor, is also larger than that ancestor. In addition to the chromosomal changes leading to larger size there have been others that result in somewhat different body conformation and still others that effectively make the two into separate species. While the chromosomes of the horse and the donkey are still sufficiently similar so that matings between them are fertile, the offspring, mules, are not, due to difficulties in the pairing of chromosomes of somewhat different conformation.

However, the differences between Adam and his descendants and the individuals of the species *Homo erectus* were very minor indeed in terms of chromosome conformation. As a result, individuals of the two types, *Homo erectus* and *Homo sapiens*, could have mated freely with no appreciable lowering of fertility. That means, in a technical sense, that they were not separate species.

Other Sources of Evolutionary Change

However, as the science of molecular genetics developed it became apparent that there are several other types of mutations besides those affecting a single protein (that is, point mutations). These are due to larger alterations in the chromosomes themselves, or even changes in the number of chromosomes.

For instance, one type of chromosome duplication, well known to gardeners, is polyploidy, in which there can be doubling, tripling, or even larger multiplications of the entire chromosome complement, usually with concomitant increases of the size of flowers or fruit. The wheat that goes into our bread and pasta, for instance, is hexaploid. That is, it has three times as many pairs of chromosomes as the diploid wild grass from which it evolved. Such mutations involving entire sets of chromosomes probably do not exist in a viable form among higher animals.

Inversions involve a reversal of the position of a chromosome segment; and fusions combine two nonhomologous chromosomes as one. Translocations arise when two nonhomologous chromosomes exchange segments. There are also deficiencies, where portions of a chromosome are lost, and duplications, where a part of a chromosome is repeated.

Such larger changes can result in sudden and dramatic mutations. However, many if not most of these result in an embryo that does not implant or a freak organism that does not survive. In other cases, the organism survives but its fertility is limited due to difficulties in the pairing up of its chromosomes with those in the remainder of the population.

However, duplications of a single chromosome or just part of a chromosome do occur among animals, including humans. A significant point regarding the "Adam" mutation is that when chromosomal rearrangements, such as insertions of bits of chromosomal material within a gene or doubling of chromosome segments, occur on the X-chromosome, the decrease in fertility tends to be much less severe than if the same thing had happened on an autosome. Had Adam's mutation been on one of the autosomes, he might have been nothing more than an early miscarriage had he been conceived at all. Or, had he been born, he may very well have been unable to function adequately or to reproduce.

Gene Doubling and Evolution

Before the discovery of the effects of certain repeating portions of DNA, it seemed that doubling of a small section of a chromosome, converting the doubled section into a controlling gene, was the most likely basis for the "Adam" mutation. There are several reasons for this.

For one thing, it is a common evolutionary event, and one that can affect growth patterns. In my own work, for instance, I came across a family in which there was a hereditary translocation that resulted in the doubling of a fairly large section of chromosome 9 in some of the individuals (Lewandowski, Yunis, Lehrke, O'Leary, Swaiman, and Sanchez, 1976). In this case the persons who inherited a doubled portion of the chromosome were only mildly handicapped, but most such doublings have very serious consequences, both mental and physical. Furthermore, the doubled section often interferes with the pairing of chromosomes at meiosis, and the result is often a reduction of fertility.

Within the past year or two, as this is written, scientists investigating a variety of neurological diseases have found a somewhat different kind of chromosomal mutation. It was first found by people searching for a means of diagnosing the genetic disorder, Huntington's disease (formerly called Huntington's chorea), before actual symptoms appeared, so that assessment of genetic risks for children of Huntington's patients would be possible.

What these researchers found was that in persons who had the gene for Huntington's disease, there was a "stutter" causing excessive growth of the control genes coding for the starting and stopping of the transcription of certain structural genes. In effect, the extra molecules caused communications between the chromosome and certain developing cells to fail.

Recent studies (Travis, 1995) have uncovered several other genetic disorders of the type, including spinocerebellar ataxia Type 1 and dentorubal and pallidoluysian atrophy. Even more than the genes for such diseases, Adam's mutation was a rare event since it had a positive instead of a negative effect, so that it increased instead of decreased the survival capacity of those who inherited it. Being on the X-chromosome, it would have a much smaller effect on the fertility of those carrying the gene; and, even more important from an evolutionary standpoint, the changed phenotype would show up in full force in the first male to inherit the gene, thus giving evolutionary forces a chance to work on it immediately.

Evolutionary Effects of Duplicated Genes

There are undoubtedly many mechanisms by which the phenotypic changes occur as a result of chromosomal alterations. While it is tempting to ascribe

the changes in the development of Adam's central nervous system to a greater amount of chromosomal material (more genes, more growth), it is more
accurate to say that changes in growth patterns occur when the amount of
chromosomal material between a structural gene and its regulatory gene is
altered (Goodenough, 1978). Up to a certain point, the greater the greater
the change, the greater the effect.

Moreover, it is frequently the case that even though the original portion
of a doubled or decreased section may have been a *structural* gene, relating
to the nature of a particular protein, the duplicate area may take on a *regulatory* function. As Volpe (1981, p. 179) says: "When loci are duplicated,
the duplicated DNA sequences need not evolve into structural genes. Indeed, during the course of evolution, several, or even many, of the duplicated loci may have become new regulatory genes".

However, the hypothesized "Adam" gene was not such a doubling. It
may, in fact, have been a deletion. Recent findings reported by Travis
(1995) suggest that there is an extensive repetition of a single nucleotide,
which operates as a controlling gene for the growth pattern of the neurones
related to intellectual functioning, and that there is an optimal range of
frequencies for that sequence (American College of Medical Genetics, 1996).
Apparently, the type of mental defect associated with a change in that frequency is due to an *excess* of nucleotides.

Because that controlling element is so new, in an evolutionary sense, it
has not yet stabilized and so is subject to frequent remutations. Further
doublings or deletions would affect the expression of the "Adam" gene. This
would cause mental subnormality in most cases, although (as will be discussed later) it may also result in an occasional genius.

In effect, there may have been a "stutter" during the formation of Adam's
X-chromosome, so that a change occurred in the frequency of a certain
three-nucleotide section. As a result, he probably ended up with something
in the range of 6 to 50 repeats of the triad, CGG (cytosine-guanine-guanine),
located between a certain regulatory and a structural gene. That is the number found in most people today (American College of Medical Genetics,
1996).

In summary, an alteration of a repeated chromosomal segment on the X-
chromosome has now been identified with X-linked mental retardation. It
is a cluster of nucleotide triplets like those that would ordinarily code for an
amino acid, but in this case it seems to be a regulatory gene, not a structural
one (Travis, 1995; American College of Medical Genetics, 1996). The frequency of its occurrence at the particular site involved has a relationship to
the extent of development of that part of the nervous system related to intellectual abilities. It would seem that indirectly, but very positively, this group
of nucleotides codes for IQ!

The original "Adam" mutation, then, was probably due to a change in the number of CGG segments in a critical area of his X-chromosome. A reversion to the primitive pattern of inserted segments in Adam's descendants could upset the growth pattern for the part of the brain related to intellectual functioning, which would in turn result in mental deficiency of the type now commonly called "fragile-X syndrome". This is discussed further in chapter 12.

In addition, changes in closely related chromosomal areas could similarly affect other, noncognitive, abilities, leading to learning disorders and other special disabilities. This subject is discussed further in chapter 13.

Chapter 4

Chromosomes, Especially X

Hypothesis 1. A significant mutation related to the growth or development of the parts of the brain involved with cognitive and language ability occurred on the X-chromosome of an individual of the species *Homo erectus*.

The instructions for building a human being—a specific one, not just a human being in general—are contained in 46 tiny bodies found in the nucleus of almost every cell of the body. (The red blood cells are the major exception). Each such set of chromosomes is a duplicate of the one formed at conception, when the half-set in the egg from the mother is paired up with a half-set from a sperm of the father. The new set of chromosomes thus formed splits into two identical ones, and each of those in turn splits, and so on, over and over.

As a rough estimate, there are probably far in excess of 100 billion sets of chromosomes just in the human brain, which is only a small portion of the body (Lafee, 1995). Each set contains a complete set of instructions for building the human in which they occur. They are incredibly tiny. In fact, the complete blueprints for every person now living—a set of chromosomes from each of over 5 billion people—could be packed into a pellet much smaller than an aspirin tablet. Most of the instructions are the same between individuals. Less than 1 percent of the genes account for all of the multitudinous differences between persons.

About 94 percent of the instructions in each set are in, or on, the autosomes, those 44 chromosomes found in pairs, one from each parent, in both males and females (figure 4-1). It is with the other 6 percent, those on the sex chromosomes, with which we are primarily concerned here.

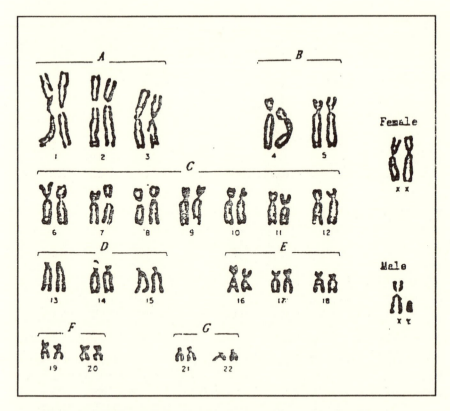

Figure 4-1. Human chromosomes in karyogram form. The first 22 pairs are the same for both sexes.

The Sex Chromosomes

Half of the people in the world, the females, are lucky enough to have two of the medium-sized X-chromosomes. They're called that, not because of their shape during one stage of mitosis, but because the committee in charge of nomenclature wanted to distinguish them from the autosomes, which are assigned numbers.

The males are not so lucky. They get only one X-chromosome plus a tiny Y-chromosome. On the X-chromosomes are many genetic instructions relating to every organ system in the body. As far as anyone knows for sure, the only important functions of the genes on the Y-chromosome are for maleness and to compensate for the lack of a second X-chromosome. If you've got a Y, you're a guy.

This system is great for seeing that there's a guy for every gal, and vice versa, since one would expect that in splitting up into half sets in the process called meiosis, half of the groups of chromosomes going into the sperm would have an X-chromosome and half, a Y. In effect, half of the sperms would produce girls, and half boys. (Note that it is the father's sperm that determines the sex of the child. The mother has nothing to do with it).

And technically, that's the way it is. However, for some reason (maybe because they're lighter and can travel faster) more Y-bearing sperms fertilize eggs than X-bearing. At conception, it is estimated by some experts that there are about 35 percent more boys started than girls.

The Weaker Sex?

Even from conception, males are not as tough as the so-called weaker sex. By the time of birth, so many more male than female fetuses have failed to implant or have otherwise died off that there are only about 5 or 6 percent more boys than girls born. Even then the disadvantage to the poor males doesn't stop. Except for the diseases specific to females, just about everything in the sickness line hits males harder than females. By the age of 40 there are about the same numbers of men and women, and from then on it gets worse and worse. At the senior citizens' singles societies there are likely to be a half dozen unattached females for every available male, which is great odds for dirty old men, or for those widowers looking for someone to nurse them through their last years. Census figures show that in the United States women live, on an average, more than 7 years longer than men (U.S. Bureau of the Census, 1990, table 103).

A large part of this difference goes back, directly or indirectly, to genes on the X-chromosome. Take another look at figure 4-1. Suppose a girl or woman has a defective gene on one of her X-chromosomes, say a gene that results in inadequate clotting of blood following an injury. No problem. The chances are that the comparable gene on the other X-chromosome is all right, so although the females may bleed more severely than average, on the whole it's not serious.

But what if a fellow has that same defective gene? He doesn't have a second X-chromosome to straighten things out, so he does have a problem. It's called hemophilia, the bleeders' disease, and without modern medical care the boy can bleed to death from the slightest injury.

The same thing applies to a greater or lesser degree to scores of other conditions, including some serious diseases. In some cases the genes for the disease are on the X-chromosome. In others, that chromosome has genes that lead to a predisposition to a disorder. For instance, in 1986 almost two and a half times as many men as women died of heart disease (U.S. Bureau of the Census, 1989, table 118). That excess of males with problems likewise applies to many other characteristics that are not primarily physical, including mental disorders and *deficits in IQ* (Lehrke, 1972a; 1974; 1978).

Xs and IQs

Let's take IQ. Suppose a girl has a somewhat defective gene for the development of IQ on one of her X-chromosomes. Chances are that the comparable gene on the other X-chromosome is better. In effect, the good gene counteracts the bad one, or at least it averages out with the bad one.

But what about the male who has the same defective gene on his X-chromosome? He doesn't have a second X-chromosome to average things out, so he's mentally subnormal. Depending on how one defines the term and what population one studies, there are somewhere between 25 and 90 percent more mentally subnormal males than females.

There are also many times more boys with specific reading and arithmetic disorders, even though they may be of normal intelligence otherwise. And many more boys than girls have a problem in learning what parents, teachers, and others consider right and proper, so they present problems of behavior. Table 4.1, most of which was adapted from publications of Dr. Arthur Jensen, shows some of the areas where boys are worse off than girls.

The Other Side of the Coin

Fortunately for the lads, there's another side to the coin. Suppose that a girl has a particularly good gene for IQ on one of her X-chromosomes. Then, according to the law of averages (or the law of regression to the mean, if you want to be technical) the other one is likely to be less good, and so she tends to go down toward average.

But what about a boy? Suppose he has that particularly good gene on his X-chromosome. That's it. He's very smart, unless something happens to damage his brain somewhere along the line.

That's what happened to Adam. As a result of a mix-up in his mother's X-chromosomes, he inherited a set of genes that acted in such a way that the nerve connections in part of his brain, and consequently his intelligence, developed more rapidly and for many more years than was the case for the people around him. Since he didn't have another X-chromosome with genes to counteract the good ones, he was exceptionally bright and therefore exceptionally able to survive and reproduce.

Table 4.1. Male : female ratios for
various forms of disability

Behavior problems	9.4 : 1
Reading disorders	8.0 : 1
Delinquency	4.5 : 1
Pre-delinquency	3.4 : 1
Personality disorders	2.6 : 1
School failure	2.6 : 1
Mental disease	2.3 : 1
Special class placement	1.7 : 1
Mental subnormality	1.5 : 1

What Happened to Adam's Children?

However, Adam's children weren't so lucky. The boys inherited his Y-chromosome and there was nothing remarkable about that. Fortunately, the supergene wasn't lost, since all of his girls received a duplicate of it. However, because of the way the sex chromosomes work, the girls probably weren't much brighter than their brothers.

But, half of *their* sons would have inherited the new gene and so would have been very bright, like their grandfather. Half of their daughters would have received it also, to pass along to their sons and daughters. It wasn't until one of the new type of males mated with a female descendant of Adam, one who happened to carry the new gene, that it was possible for a girl child of theirs to inherit two of the superior X-chromosomes—a girl who would be as bright as her bright brothers. In short, it took a while before the bright girls arrived on the scene, but when they did they undoubtedly used their superior ability to take particularly good care of their children, so that they were more likely than most to survive and have children of their own; and most important of all, to pass on their superior gene for intelligence.

The Lyon Hypothesis

A question that might be asked, and in fact it was asked for years, is, "If a woman has two X-chromosomes and a man only one, why doesn't she have twice as much of all the traits on the X-chromosome as a man does?" For instance, why aren't women twice as smart as men?

The person who finally figured out the answer was Dr. Mary P. Lyon (1962), who showed that in each of those cells in a female's body having chromosomes (virtually all of them except the red blood cells), one of the X-chromosomes is effectively turned off. That is, the instructions on it have little or no effect, so overall only one X-chromosome per cell is on the job.

What has happened is that a couple of weeks after conception something happens within the cells that causes one or the other of the X-chromosomes to become inert. All future descendants of each cell will have the same X-chromosome, either the one inherited from the father or the one inherited from the mother, set off to one side. In fact, these Barr bodies, as the turned-off X-chromosomes are called, can be seen under a microscope.

Thus, a female's cells are a mixture, or more aptly, a mosaic. In one little clump the paternal X-chromosome will remain active, and in the next one, the maternal. In some cases it is possible to see the results of this mosaicism. For instance, scientists have taken photographs of the eye grounds (the back of the eye where the retina is located) of a woman who inherited the X-linked disorder of ocular albinism from one of her parents. The retina showed a mixture of clumps of the normal black cells and of abnormal albino ones. The woman's vision was somewhat deficient, but she wasn't blind, as a boy who inherited the genes for ocular albinism would be.

It should be noted that if one of the X-chromosomes is physically abnormal, such as having either an excess or a deficiency of material, this tends to be the one that is turned off in all of a woman's somatic cells. However, that doesn't apply to the ova (egg cells). Either the normal or abnormal X-chromosome has an equal chance of being selected. There have been instances in which women had an X-chromosome with extra or deleted material. In such cases the woman herself has usually been normal, since the defective chromosome was turned off in all cells. However, when these women had sons, those who had inherited the defective X-chromosome were abnormal, if they survived to be born.

Evolution via the X-Chromosome

From an evolutionary standpoint, the position of the "Adam" gene on the X-chromosome was particularly fortunate, since the carriers experienced little or no decrease in fertility. Further, the gene did not have to be matched up with another for it to be fully effective. Being on the X-chromosome, the gene would be expressed by any male who inherited it, and evolutionary selection could start at once. It was, as my mentor, Dr. John F. Opitz, once said, "a most unusual gene" (Opitz, 1986, p. 1).

Chapter 5

Mutations

Hypothesis 2. The mutation was probably due to a change in the number of nucleotides (a fairly common evolutionary event) in a small area of an egg-producing cell of a woman who lived about 200,000 years ago. By particularly fortunate chance, the site of the mutation was on the X-chromosome rather than on one of the autosomes, with the result that the consequent phenotypic changes would be expressed immediately in any male to receive the mutant chromosome. It would not, however, be fully expressed in a female unless she had inherited the mutant gene from both parents.

Mutations

Adam was a mutant. That is, something had affected his genetic instructions in a way that caused him to develop in a manner that was different from his ancestors and those about him. In addition, he could pass these new instructions on to his descendants.

By particularly fortunate chance, the site of Adam's mutation was on the X-chromosome rather than on one of the autosomes, with the result that the resulting phenotypic changes would be expressed immediately in any male to receive the mutant chromosome. It would not, however, be fully expressed in a female unless she had inherited the mutant gene from both parents.

This mutation was unusual in that it was highly advantageous for Adam's survival and reproduction. Most aren't. In fact this particular mutation was so favorable that it led to a new subspecies within the order of primates, a subspecies that now almost certainly encompasses all living people.

That he should have a mutation, in general, isn't at all surprising. From evidence based on the mutation rates of fruit flies, mice, bacteria, and other organisms, it would not be surprising if many, if not most, people have one or more new mutations in their genetic makeup. It is only when such new mutations show up as some unusual and obvious condition in a person or in his or her descendants that we become aware of them. Such mutations involve an extremely large number of conditions, including diseases such as tuberous sclerosis, hemophilia, achondroplasia, and phenylketonuria. These are examples of conditions that limit survival and reproduction to such an extent that they would have long ago disappeared from the genetic pool had it not been for recurring new mutations.

Most mutations, on the other hand, probably have no evolutionary effect whatever. The genetic codes that call for each of the amino acids that go into the building of a protein can have as many as six different forms. As far as we know, a mutation that results in the substitution of one of these codes for another has no effect.

In other cases, the effect of a change is not obvious unless both chromosomes of a pair carry it. The gene for sickle cell anemia (type S hemoglobin) is only one chemical different from the coding for normal hemoglobin. The person who has this slightly changed instruction on just one of his or her haploid (half) sets of chromosomes is not harmed by it. In fact, such a person has the advantage of being more than usually resistant to malaria.

However, a child who inherits the gene for type S hemoglobin from both parents, so that he or she has no red blood cells with normal hemoglobin, is seriously and painfully ill and will usually die young. Thus, if a mutant gene, like that for sickle cell anemia, is of the autosomal recessive type, it may be passed on for many generations before it ever shows up in both chromosomes of a pair. In fact, many such genes are undoubtedly lost, simply not passed along somewhere in the early generations after its first occurrence, and never show up at all. In some cases, such as the one for Type S (sickle cell) hemoglobin, a mutation can be both harmful and helpful, depending upon whether an individual has one or two genes carrying it.

On the whole, though, the great majority of new mutations that are not simply neutral are harmful. For one thing, humans and their subhuman ancestors have spent millions of years in the process of becoming adapted to life on this planet, and most favorable mutations have already occurred and been preserved. Those that are not favorable have generally been weeded out by evolutionary selection, although they can recur. In general, then, only genes that result in increased fitness, or are essentially neutral, have remained in the population. The chances that any new mutation will do more good than harm are relatively small, and the chances that a mutation will do a *great deal* more good than harm are almost infinitesimal.

Pleiotropy

For another thing, most genes that can be clearly evaluated are pleiotropic. That is, they affect several organ systems. The chances that the changes introduced by a mutant gene can be fitted into several existing organ systems without disruption of at least one function are not too great. For instance, there is a very common mutant gene in the human population that was particularly helpful to some of our ancestors who lived in a situation where the food supply was highly variable, as between summer and winter. One effect of that gene was to help persons build up fat deposits during the good times, which then helped them avoid starvation during the bad times.

However, under less stressful conditions, that gene results in oversize babies that often die at birth, loss of mothers in childbirth, slow healing of wounds, excessive infections, and inability to utilize some excellent sources of carbohydrates. We call it diabetes.

Thus, Adam's mutation was a most unusual one. It created a condition, increased intelligence, that was helpful in both personal survival and in increased chances for reproduction. It occurred in such a way that any increase in head size appeared after the babies were safely born; otherwise, he and others like him might have had heads too large to pass safely through the birth canal. It did not result in any changes in his anatomy beyond what his existing system was able to accommodate. For instance, if his brain now required more room as he grew older, the increase was well within the skull's capability for growth, without crowding or damage to other organs. It did not require any substantial increase in blood flow that might have resulted in his heart and circulatory system being incapable of meeting the need. It was an almost perfect mutation, and it occurred at an evolutionary stage when the physical structure of the body was ready for it.

There is a chance, suggested by clinical findings regarding certain boys with X-linked mental retardation, that there was a pleiotropic effect of the mutation which, like the others, did not have enough effect on the reproductive potential of the new type of male to offset the undoubted advantage of higher intellectual capabilities. That effect was a substantial reduction in the size of the testes.

Certainly there is no archeological evidence of such a soft-tissue difference between the old and the new type of male. What we have is a finding that affected males in families with a certain type of X-linked mental deficiency (further discussed in chapter 12) often have unusually large testes. Now there is a substantial likelihood that the type of mental defect found in these families is essentially a throwback to *Homo erectus*; and if that is the case, it *may* be that the large testes are also a throwback, due to pleiotropic effects of the same mutation that caused the increased growth of the connections within the brain.

It is not certain how prevalent the phenomenon of megalotestes is among men with X-linked mental subnormality. It was not noted in any of the families I, personally, studied, but that may be because neither I nor the physicians with whom I worked bothered to look. The phenomenon was brought to my attention by Drs. Brian and Gillian Turner (1974) of Australia, who reported some cases. There have been other similar reports in the medical literature, for instance that of Drs. Ruvalcaba, Mhyre, Roosen-Runge, and Beckwith (1977) whose cases came from the State of Washington.

A Quantum Leap?

Geneticists have tended to discount the possibility of a sudden, or quantum, leap from *Homo erectus*, as many scientists have labeled our final evolutionary ancestor, to *Homo sapiens*, or modern Man, because of the likelihood of such pleiotropic effects. However, in a purely physiological sense, Adam's mutation was not a big jump. While there may have been some secondary effects, the main mutation was not a particularly great one. It simply changed the signals for the starting, stopping, and rate of growth of a particular group of *parts* of cells—the axons and/or dendrites of some brain neurones. In other words, it increased the interconnections between certain brain cells by causing the connecting fibers to grow more rapidly and for a much longer period of time. The number of nerve cells, per se, was not affected. Adam, like babies today, presumably had all of his brain cells by the fifth month of gestation. Any growth after that was in the nerve fibers and endings, and most of that occurred after he was safely born so that there would be no problem of his head being able to pass through the birth canal.

Types of Mutations

Mutations, in general, occur by many different processes. A full discussion of these would fill many books, but there is a good summary in a book edited by Francisco Ayala (1976) called *Molecular Evolution*. The particular method hypothesized for the present theory is that of an insertion of chromosomal material between the genes controlling the production of the proteins(s) needed for nerve growth and the output of those genes, possibly messenger RNA. In his book, *Complex Adaptations in Evolving Populations*, T. H. Frazetta (1975, p. 93) has pointed out that numerous authors have discussed how such duplications could provide the genetic basis for complex-appearing evolutionary changes.

The evolutionary effects of the enlargement of a section of a chromosome are many. For one thing, such doubling could permit one section to continue its vital functions while the other was available for new mutations that might result in entirely new functions. As previously mentioned, Volpe (1981) pointed out that when duplications occur, regardless of the role of the original part, the new section can take on a different function. It can be, for instance, a regulatory rather than a structural gene.

However, it is now becoming apparent that deletions can have similar effects. This seems to be what happened in Adam's case. That is, the change affected a gene controlling the production of a protein needed for building neuronal interconnections and having, as is usual, built into it genes regulating the starting and stopping of the process.

The mutation, then, would simply have resulted in a change in the growth signals, causing the tissue involved to remain youthful, in the sense of its continuing to grow, for a longer period. Such genetic changes are called neotenous, which might be defined as a type of evolutionary change in which the youthful, or even fetal, stages of development of a part of an organism persist until a much greater stage of maturity. This process is further described in chapter 6.

Chromosome Doubling or Deletion and Fertility

Most changes caused by the doubling or deletion of a section of a chromosome must create a marked improvement in the organism's functioning if the change is to persist. That is because chromosomes, especially autosomes, with abnormal amounts of material can cause partial sterility. Even if there is no marked effect on the first generation, there can be delayed effects. For instance, substantial differences in the amount and chromosomal location of genetic instructions can produce sterility in the offspring, as in hybrids of the horse and ass to produce a mule.

But, as previously mentioned, such differences in the amount of chromosomal material passed on by the male and female parents do not have a comparably severe effect when they are on the X-chromosome. And, of course, the mutation being discussed did, indeed, have a strong selective advantage—more than enough to offset a moderate reproductive handicap.

At the present point in evolution, many duplications or deletions of chromosomes or parts of them are lethal, in a genetic sense. That is, they result in decreased reproduction. In fact, they are often lethal in the more usual sense unless, by rare chance, they happen to involve a function that is not essential to survival. For instance, the mutation which resulted in the loss of the ability to synthesize vitamin C in the body, which occurred in our prehumanoid simian ancestors and which still exists in modern Man, was not

44   The X-Factor

critical because humans and their close simian relatives ordinarily have a diet that provides enough of it anyway. (If they don't, they suffer from a serious disease called scurvy).

However, the inability to synthesize an amino acid called tyrosine, resulting in the genetic disease called phenylketonuria, often results in such severe mental handicap that the person is unlikely to reproduce. And even if a female phenylketonuric does reproduce, her children are virtually always too severely handicapped to have children.

In Adam's case the mutation on the X-chromosome was favorable enough to more than offset whatever minor problems it might have created, and so it spread rapidly within the small groups which included his descendants. It was on the X-chromosome, so that it didn't greatly affect fertility. In effect, it was a most remarkable mutation, unlikely to have occurred separately for each racial group of Man.

Chapter 6

Neoteny

Hypothesis 3. By nature, the mutation was neotenous. That is, its effect was to maintain a youthful characteristic, that of continued growth of certain connections within the brain, for an extended period, by comparison with that of others of the species *Homo* alive at the time.

One of my earlier papers on the X-linkage of major intellectual traits, published in the *American Journal of Mental Deficiency* (Lehrke, 1972a, p. 611), started out, "It is hypothesized that major genes relating to intelligence are located on the X-chromosome. Apparently these genes relate to certain verbal abilities and to perception of spatial relationships." Nothing was said about the nature of these genes—about how they actually influenced intellectual functioning—but I assumed that somehow or other they affected the basic physical structure of the parts of the brain involved with those traits.

To me, this idea was given some impetus by the knowledge that one X-linked gene, or set of genes, does indeed have a major effect on the structure of the brain. That is the X-linked gene which, when mutated, results in the Edwards type of hydrocephalus. This condition involves abnormalities of growth of the area surrounding the Aqueduct of Sylvius, near the back of the brain, and leads to hydrocephaly, mental deficiency, and spasticity.

That was just a hunch, with many things going against it, so I simply steered clear of the subject. However, Dr. Anne Anastasi of Fordham University, among others, noted the lack and called me on it (Anastasi, 1972), as did Doctors Nance and Engel (1972). It was Dr. Anastasi, in particular, who suggested that if the overall theory was to be made credible, some explanation of the nature of the gene was in order.

The problem became more obvious when I received a preliminary report on some studies done by Dr. Steve Vandenberg and his students at the University of Colorado. This group studied the inheritance of what might be called "micro-traits" related to intelligence. These showed no particular tendency toward X-linkage. Thus it seemed clear that whatever it was on the X-chromosome that had such important effects on intelligence was not highly localized. It was something involving almost the total function of a major portion of the brain, not some small anatomical or biochemical feature. In fact, Dr. Spearman's g, or general factor of intelligence, well known to psychology students of past generations, might appropriately have been labeled the X-factor.

Interestingly enough, Dr. Vandenberg (1962) in some earlier research had shown that such a general factor was more highly heritable than the parts of it. In other words, with some exceptions, it is the overall level of brightness rather than specific intellectual skills that is most obviously passed on from parent to child. Furthermore, autopsies and physical studies on persons with the type of X-linked mental subnormality that started this whole study (see chapter 12) showed no significant physical abnormalities except smaller than average head size in many cases. There was apparently no disease of metabolism or abnormality of physical structure, nothing that would differentiate the mentally deficient boys and men in these families from their normal or bright brothers, uncles, cousins, and nephews except the low IQ. Later on, however, there were reports that under certain conditions the X-chromosomes of some victims of non-specific X-linked mental retardation would fragment when being grown in a nutrient-deficient culture medium. The phenomenon, which is now called the "fragile-X," will be considered further in chapter 12.

The Concept of Neoteny

Even while writing the original material on X-linked mental subnormality I was becoming aware that the gene, whatever it did, was probably somehow related to an evolutionary process. In correspondence with several graduate students who had written me about my published papers I had thrown in the gratuitous suggestion that the X-linked gene was probably the basis for the evolution of *Homo erectus* to *Homo sapiens*. But that still didn't give me any clue as to the nature of the mutation.

It wasn't until I stumbled upon the concept of neoteny in an article about Desmond Morris's (1967) book, *The Naked Ape*, that the answer became clear. I had been thinking only in terms of genetic instructions relating to the structure or metabolic functioning of the temporal area of the brain, not for such a simple thing as growth controlling factors. I should have realized that organic structure is a direct consequence of the pattern of growth.

The idea of a neotenous (growth-extending) mutation had not occurred to me simply because the word and its accompanying concept wasn't in my vocabulary. Admittedly it should have been, but somehow I had missed it.

A neotenous mutation might be described as one that causes a youthful characteristic of an organism to continue beyond its usual time. For example, the penguin is able to survive in the icy waters of the Antarctic seas because, as a result of a neotenous mutation millions of years ago, it retains the downy growth with which all birds are hatched throughout its life. It doesn't shed this down in favor of feathers, as most birds do. It just grows more nice, warm, water-resistant down.

In fact, the idea of neoteny as related to Man's intellectual development, which seemed at the time to be such a dramatic discovery, wasn't even a new one, as I later learned. Dr. Ashley Montagu (1962, p. 341) had said: "The juvenile ape is more educable than the adult ape, and the suggestion here is that the preservation of the educability of the juvenile ape into the adult stage, by neoteny, serves to explain the evolution of a brain capable of being a human mind."

It was his opinion, though, that these evolutionary changes were gradual: "It is questionable whether the shift from ape to hominid status was saltatory either for morphological or for mental traits." In that he was probably correct as far as morphological traits were concerned, but there was the one dramatic leap that occurred later—that from *Homo erectus* to *Homo sapiens*.

In fact, there is evidence that the *total* changes from an ape-like creature to Man did take a long time, in terms of human lifespans, but they were still remarkably rapid in terms of evolutionary time. Dr. Montagu (1962) accounts for this rapidity of evolution by pointing out that many of the changes were neotenous.

The very important opposable thumb of Man, which is larger in humans than even the largest apes, and the angle of the skull to the spine that permits Man's upright posture are examples of fetal traits carried over to an entire life span. The growth of the skull is dependent on the size of the brain, not vice versa as many people believe, so it is not strictly speaking a neotenous trait. However, the increase in the size of the brain prior to *Homo erectus* probably was.

Head Size and Intelligence

It must be emphasized, however, that the mutation calling for overall larger brain and head size was not the same as that which resulted in the tremendous expansion of intellectual capabilities. Although the genetic capability for a reasonably large brain probably had to be present before the last dramatic mutation could take place, a big brain does not, per se, mean higher intelligence. If it did, men would almost always be smarter than women.

As a matter of fact, head sizes as large as, or even larger than, those of modern Man have been found in many prehistoric individuals. For instance, in many cases the skulls of Neanderthal Man that have been dug up were as large as those of modern Man, suggesting that in these cases the original possessors of those skulls were probably European descendants of Adam.

About 100,000 to 200,000 years after the probable origin of *Homo sapiens*, that is, about 30,000 years ago, the even larger-headed Cro-Magnon Man appeared, probably an offshoot of the Neanderthal strain. Some of their skulls were relatively huge in size, with capacities of about 1550 cc. compared with an average for modern Man of less than 1400 cc. Bones and artifacts tell us that Cro-Magnon Man was a remarkable physical specimen with such an exceptionally high level of technology for his time that he had been widely accepted as the ancestor of modern Man. Under the "Adam" theory, however, he would have been just an offshoot of the *Homo sapiens* family, but one that died out or was assimilated into other groups.

Nonetheless, recent studies have shown that, as might be expected, differences in the growth of those neurones related to intellectual functioning (the Adam mutation) are to a slight degree reflected in the size of certain areas of the brain as well as intelligence (Andreasen, Flaum, Swayze, O'Leary, Alliger, Cohen, Ehrhardt, and Yuh, 1993). (However, head sizes more than 3 standard deviations either below or above the mean are usually associated with mental subnormality).

Actually, a very recent development in the field is some evidence of significant correlations between the volume of certain brain areas, as determined by magnetic resonance imaging, and IQ (Andreasen, Flaum, Swayze, O'Leary, Alliger, Cohen, Ehrhardt, and Yuh, 1993). The subjects of the study were 37 male and 30 female adults. In the study, height was used as a correction factor, to compensate for differences in the body sizes of the subjects which would be reflected in brain size. These researchers found statistically significant correlations between the volume of several parts of the brain and IQs on the Wechsler Adult Intelligence Scale—Revised.

However, the researchers tempered the implications of the study with a caution.

> First, the modest nature of the relationships must be emphasized. Significant correlations ranged from 0.36 to 0.56, indicating that between 12% and 31% of the variance can be accounted for by the size of the brain or its subregions. This is a relatively small amount of variance, and we must conclude that although size may be among the factors related to human intelligence, many other factors must also be important. What accounts for the remainder of this variance? This particular study cannot address that question. In all likelihood, however, the answer resides in aspects of brain structure that

reflect "quality" rather than "quantity" of brain tissue: complexity of circuitry, dendritic expansion, number of synapses, thickness of myelin, metabolic efficiency, or efficiency of neurotransmitter production, release, and reuptake. (pp. 132-133)

In other words, it could be that a small part of the variability in IQ could be accounted for by a substrate involving the sheer number and size of cells. The remainder, "the aspects that reflect 'quality' rather than 'quantity,'" may very well involve the "Adam" mutation—that is, more extensive inter-connections of the neurones. This, of course, would result in enlargement of some parts of the brain.

While there were no psychologists around to determine the adult mental level of *Homo erectus* individuals, it is probable that they reached their peak of mental development long before they reached physical maturity. This is unlike modern Man, in whom the growth periods coincide to a substantial degree. Language development in *Homo erectus* probably didn't exceed that of today's average 4- or 5-year-old, especially when it came to abstract ideas and conceptual thinking. This is completely speculative, to be sure, but their ability to make and use tools makes it certain that these early hominids were considerably brighter than the modern chimpanzee, whose final mental age, not taking speech into account, is about that of a 3-year-old child. Those aspects of verbal and cognitive ability that are the exclusive characteristic of modern Man depend on the number and complexity of the neuronal connections within the brain, not on the number of brain cells.

Development of the Brain

At birth, the human baby's brain weighs about 350 grams, and it grows to about 1375 grams at maturity. At 3 years, when the chimpanzee's brain has reached its maximum size, the human's brain has reached only 81 percent of its final weight. It continues to grow and develop internally for about 15 more years, on an average. None of this growth includes the addition of any new nerve cells. They have all been present since the fifth month of gestation. What happens after that is a proliferation of the fibrous interconnections between existing neurones. It is probably the duration and complexity of the growth of such interconnections that is the difference between modern Man (starting with Adam) and his evolutionary ancestors.

Because of the high value our society places on verbal and cognitive abilities it has been difficult for anthropologists to believe that the change from a dull, though human, individual with a mental age of 5 or so years (by our standards) to modern Man could have been triggered by a single mutation. Yet, that's probably what happened.

The difference between *Homo sapiens* and his predecessor, *Homo erectus*, and probably the difference between normal persons and some present-day mentally subnormal individuals, seems to lie in a final development of nerve connections within the brain. In chimpanzees, the brain has reached almost full adult size at three years. Although the chimp can and does continue to learn new things after the end of brain growth, the complexity of its intellectual processes has reached its limit at about that time.

Although new learning doesn't stop, the *average* person reaches his or her full mental capabilities at about the age of 18. Dull persons tend to stop developing mentally before this, and brighter persons to continue beyond, a few of them for up to another 6 years or so. During this period the capabilities of the brain, as well as the amount of learning, continue to increase. As no new nerve cells have developed within the brain after 5 months gestational age, all of this mental development must be due to increased interconnections between existing cells. Without the "Adam" mutation, the development of interconnections would have stopped at maybe 5 years of age.

Chapter 7

Variability in Intelligence

Hypothesis 4. Being an aneuploid, or unbalanced, type of chromosomal event, the new mutation was unstable, since it resulted in erratic pairing of homologous chromosomes during meiosis (the formation of chromosomal complements during the creation of new egg or
sperm cells). Because it was unstable, further variations of the original mutation occurred, resulting in considerable variation in the new
genes and in their phenotypic expression. These variations were
undoubtedly subject to evolutionary selection.

Even before Adam, some degree of variation must have existed between
individuals in communications, problem solving ability, the capability of making simple associations, responsiveness to reward and punishment (that is,
the ability to learn from experience) and, in fact, in all or most of the areas
that might be called intellectual. The effect of the new gene(s) would be not
only to enhance the level or complexity of some of these abilities but probably to amplify individual differences in them.

It should not be assumed, however, that present-day individual differences in cognitive ability simply reflect such "amplified" differences. Most would
probably be due to additional mutations at the site of the "Adam" gene(s).

This is made more likely by the fact that the primitive (pre-Adam) intellectual level, while variable, was probably more consistent between individuals than is the case today. As a matter of evolutionary selection over a period of one or two million years or so, the less favorable alleles would have
been weeded out and the more favorable ones retained.

Because of the relatively short time since Adam, evolutionary processes
have not yet reached a point of standardizing intelligence levels in modern
Man. In fact, the world's more advanced societies tend to capitalize on such

intellectual differences, since they encourage occupational specialization.

It should not be assumed, either, that all types of mental abilities were equally enhanced by the "Adam" mutation. Simple associative learning and memory were probably little improved since they must have been well established in Man's forebears. Even today, as Baumeister (1967) and others have pointed out, mentally dull persons tend to be more similar to average persons in their ability to handle associative learning than in more involved cognitive processes.

Generally it can be said that once a gene has reached a point where it meets the needs of the organism it is not likely to undergo frequent changes. While mutations affecting that gene may occur in the population, these are likely to be less satisfactory than the existing one, and so be selected against. As an example, the genetic instructions for building the protein molecule of the alpha chain of hemoglobin have undergone only two enduring changes during the total evolutionary time between Man, back to a common ancestor, and then up again to the chimpanzee, a total evolutionary distance of millions of years. In effect, the hemoglobins of Man and chimpanzees differ in only two molecules out of over 150.

The Instability of the New Genes

Why then can we assume that Adam's mutation has undergone numerous changes in the intervening couple of hundred thousands of years? It is not that the original mutation didn't fit the needs of Adam and his descendants. The main reason is the instability of those *new* mutations that result from changes in the amount of chromosomal material.

For example, in such cases frequent new mutations are likely to arise in the process of crossing over. During meiosis, the process by which haploid (half) sets of chromosomes are created for inclusion in gametes (sperms and eggs), homologous chromosomes crisscross and then recombine at the crossing sites in such a way that genes from the male and female parents are reassorted. In effect, a new chromosome is produced that includes parts of both the maternally- and paternally-derived chromosomes.

For instance, figure 7-1 shows a very simple crossing-over pattern which results in the first third being composed of paternal genes, the next third, of maternal genes, and the remainder of paternal genes. In addition, there is another chromosome with the complementary pattern. Either could end up in the sperm or egg. Such crossing-over patterns can be repeated many times, especially on the larger chromosomes.

Crossing over is a regular part of meiosis, and it has some evolutionary value by increasing the genetic heterogeneity of the offspring. Not that further heterogeneity is greatly needed. Even without crossing over, each

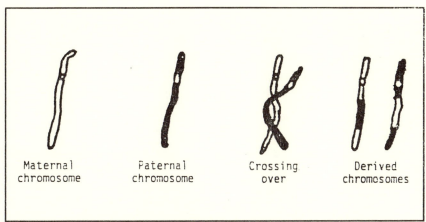

Figure 7-1. Chromosomal crossing over.

person is capable of 2^{23} types of gametes, just by different combinations of the chromosomes on his or her 23 pairs of chromosomes. In other words, a woman could have 8,388,608 genetically different types of eggs among the 400,000 with which she is born. (Fewer than 500 of these will mature sufficiently to be fertilizable). A man could have the same number of possible chromosome combinations in his sperm cells. Thus, the children of any one couple could be of over 70,000,000,000,000 genetically different types, even without crossing over—probably a few thousand times more variations than there have been individuals of the species *Homo sapiens* since Adam's time.

With the addition of crossing over, the number of possible genomes from any one person becomes virtually infinite. In addition, the crossing over process itself increases the number of potential new mutations, especially in chromosomal areas where doubling or deletion has already occurred, since imperfect matching up of the ends can result in new instances of doubling or deletion.

For example, let us take the instance of one of Adam's daughters. In the process of matching up her X-chromosomes (one from Adam and one from her mother, who would have had the smaller primitive X-chromosome) there would be a section of Adam's chromosome a bit longer than its mate. In matching up prior to crossing over, there would have been a little loop, shown in a greatly exaggerated fashion in figure 7-2.

This process is not directly observable in humans or higher animals, although it can be inferred from certain types of genetic studies, that is, linkage studies. It is, however, clearly seen under a microscope in the salivary gland chromosomes of fruit flies and certain other insects. The mismatch could affect the exact point of crossover at the ends of the loop. Also, because the loop was due to the presence of two homologous sections apposed

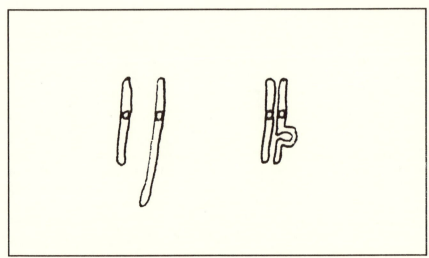

Figure 7-2. Loop formation.

to each other, crossing over might occur at some median point. That is, the crossover could occur between a point on the original chromosome and a comparable point on the doubled portion, cutting off a section of the loop and combining it with the remainder of the original chromosome. In any case, experiments with fruit flies have shown that crossovers between mutated and unmutated chromosomes tend to be erratic. A well-known example is the bar-eye phenomenon in *Drosophila* discussed later in this chapter.

Even after the breeding population of Adam's descendants consisted entirely of persons with the new-type X-chromosomes there would be further complications as doubled portions of slightly different lengths had to match up. That same situation probably exists today. In any case, the length of the portion of the X-chromosome involved in the "Adam" mutation has certainly continued to vary, right up to the present, resulting in a few cases in remutations and the start of new pedigrees of X-linked mental subnormality such as those described in chapter 12. In all probability, there are also mutations resulting in exceptional brightness.

Such chromosomal variations can not only explain the wide range of differences in individual intelligence, but they can also account for additional mutations affecting closely related parts of the brain. For instance, it is not unlikely that a secondary mutation providing further development of the other (non-dominant) half of the brain occurred as a result of additional changes in the area of the primary "Adam" mutation site. (This is further discussed in chapter 11).

The Bar-Eye Mutation

Because deletions or insertions of chromosomal material are an important source of evolutionary change, the matter deserves more attention. Perhaps the best way to make the concept clear is to use an example in which the phenomena of doubling, redoubling, and loss of doubled portions of chromosomes have actually been observed.

In *Drosophila* (fruit flies) there are bundles of chromosomes in the salivary glands which can readily be observed under a microscope. In these, the portions of chromosomes associated with many obvious mutations can often be determined by comparing the salivary chromosomes of the mutant flies with those of the normal or "wild" type.

A mutation in which the normally round eye of the fruit fly becomes much narrower (bar eye) can be seen to be due to the doubling of a small segment of the X-chromosome (see figure 7-3). This mutation, as might be expected, is relatively unstable. When bar-eye flies are mated with the wild type, with no further selection for it, the mutation tends to be lost within a few generations. Furthermore, when bar-eye flies are mated with others of

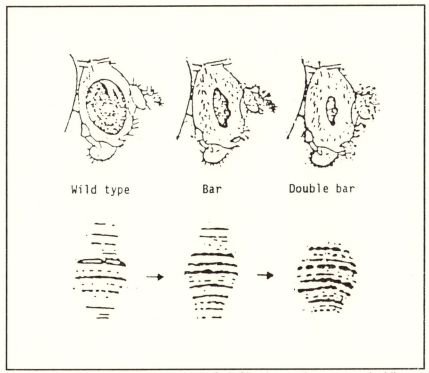

Figure 7-3. The bar-eye phenomenon in fruit flies due to chromosome doubling.

the same type there are occasional additional mutations in which the chromosome area is redoubled, resulting in an even narrower eye (double bar).

The Effects of Doubled Chromosome Areas

While it is tempting to assume that the doubling effect is due to the actual quantity of chromosomal material, what really is affected is more likely to be the physical distance between the controlling genes, those that in effect turn on and off the product of the gene, and the structural genes, which give the instructions for the building of proteins. When the separation of the structural gene from the controlling gene is altered, there is a change in the growth patterns. The greater the difference from the norm, within certain limits, the greater the effect (Goodenough, 1978).

The same types of phenomena could occur for the hypothesized area resulting in a change in the pattern of growth of neuronal interconnections within the brain. This could result in a marked change in the growth pattern leading in most cases to mental subnormality (see chapter 12), but in all likelihood there could also be changes in the positive direction, toward higher IQ (see chapter 15).

From studies of cases where X-linked mental subnormality is associated with a tendency for X-chromosomes to break up in nutrient-deficient culture media, the so called fragile-X syndrome (de la Cruz, 1985), it is probable that the site of the chromosomal abnormality is Xq27. That is, it is at locus 27, which is near the end of the long arm of the X-chromosome. (This is discussed in more detail in chapter 12.)

The implication is that because of their newness, in an evolutionary sense, the genes for greater development of the "IQ" part of the brain continue to be subject to frequent mutations or remutations. In addition, there has probably been an extension of the new growth pattern to the nondominant hemisphere, resulting in an increase in certain specialized abilities. Some of these mutations would be expected to cause mental deficits and, on rare occasions, they could also lead to exceptionally high levels of ability.

Chapter 8

Division of Labor Within the Brain

Hypothesis 5. The part of the brain most affected by the primary mutation was that portion of the temporal region related to cognitive and language functions. The basic centers for these traits were, of course, already present in a primitive form, but the mutation caused their neural interconnections to develop for a longer period of time and thus to a far greater complexity.

Wrapped around each side of the brain and extending down into the cleft between the two halves are a pair of areas that control voluntary movements of the body. Because the connections of these areas to body muscles, when plotted, correspond roughly to the shape of the body, the area is called the homunculus, or "little man". Essentially, the nerve centers in the "leg" of the homunculus control movement of the leg, etc. In general, the right half of the brain has primary control of the movements of the left half of the body, and vice versa. The two sides are so closely interconnected that this is normally not apparent, but extensive damage to the motor cortex on one side of the brain will cause at least temporary partial paralysis (hemiparesis) on the opposite side of the body.

The homunculi are not by any means a good representation of the body. The "hands", for instance, are much too large, reflecting the complexity of the nerve connections to the hands and consequent intricacy and precision of their possible movements. Even more distorted, and much too large in proportion, is the "head" area, in which are located the centers for speech, language, spatial perception, and some other primarily intellectual functions.

As mentioned, most of the nerve systems from the homuncular area cross over, with the left side of the brain controlling the right side of the body, and vice versa. However, the jaws, lips, tongue and throat—those organs pertaining to speech—are on the midline of the body, so that separate control of the two halves is limited. As a result, the temporal areas of the brain controlling speech functions have been able to evolve separately, giving each side different jobs.

In most cases, the homuncular "head" on the side controlling the dominant hand (for right handers, usually the left side) is the language area, the region in which most language-based thinking takes place. The opposite side controls the motor aspects of speech, in addition to certain special skills such as spatial perception and related logic and probably several other functions not as well defined. Certain musical and mathematical abilities are probably among them.

Evidence of Localization of Brain Function

These brain localizations have been studied by many techniques, but particularly by the follow-up of cases in which there had been accidental or surgical ablation of a particular area. If a portion of the motor area on one side of the brain is removed, there is a disruption of function of the area on the other side of the body that is controlled by that section. (A rather remarkable example of such localization is given later on in this book, at the beginning of chapter 11).

The effects of head wounds during two world wars and other more localized combats have helped refine the localization of brain functions. There are also many examples of the effects of surgery on the brain in civilian populations.

The Case of Joan

For instance, there is the case of Joan (a pseudonym), who had been a resident of a Minnesota state institution for the mentally subnormal for about 30 years when I first met her. Like many of the long-time residents of that particular institution, she had been originally committed because of epilepsy, and she remained at the institution when it was converted to a facility for the mentally subnormal.

She was a grandmotherly person, of normal appearance except for a moderate degree of left hemiplegia and a purplish birthmark that covered much of the right side of her face and temple region. That mark was due to congenital nonmalignant tumors of the blood vessels of that area (Sturge-Weber disease). Because these tumors affected not only the skin and muscles of one side of her head, but extended inward to the temporal region of her brain, she was less bright than she might otherwise have been, although not actually mentally subnormal. The tumors also caused her epilepsy.

However, these epileptic seizures were later brought under good control by some dramatic neurosurgery in which a substantial portion of the right side of her brain was removed. She continued to live in the institution for another 8 or 9 years, because it was the staff's impression that her long institutional history had made it impossible for her to function in the community. Fortunately for her, a new medical administrator came along who did not share this idea and Joan was sent to a more normal life in the community.

But while she was still institutional I had a chance to follow up on her functioning. Fortunately, before my time at the institution a sharp young psychologist had decided to find out how the brain surgery would affect her functioning. Just before the operation, Joan had been given a Stanford-Binet intelligence test, which is highly verbal in its content, and a Bender-Gestalt, a test for brain damage which involves mainly spatial perception and hand-eye co-ordination. Then both tests were repeated 6 months after surgery.

On both the pre- and post-operative tests, Joan's IQ on the Binet was in the middle 70s, or borderline. There was a slight drop between the first and second test, but no more than might have been expected by chance. The Bender-Gestalt, which involves copying simple geometric patterns, was abnormal both before and after surgery.

Seven years after the surgery I happened to give Joan the same two tests, without knowledge of her past test results. With a large part of her brain gone, she remained as high in IQ as she had been before surgery. The strange thing was that on this last test her Bender-Gestalt results were completely normal except for the signs of immaturity that would be expected on the basis of her IQ.

One would think that with the spatial perception portion of her brain gone she would have trouble doing the test, but somehow she had managed to relearn, or had learned from scratch, the perceptual and motor skills involved, using the other half of the brain. As long as she had the damaged portion, such relearning was impossible, but without it, the other half of the brain could perform the usual functions of both halves.

Other "Right-Brain" Functions

It is apparent from studies of many such cases that the right and left homuncular "heads" are physically similar and to a great extent are interchangeable in function. In fact, for many people, especially left-handers, the functions are interchanged between left and right. However, they seem to be under separate genetic control and have different patterns of growth. For instance, it is possible for a person to inherit high verbal ability (dominant hemisphere) but low spatial ability (nondominant hemisphere), or vice versa. As an example, some of the brightest young men I know as far as verbal skills are concerned, are total washouts when it comes to simple spatial and mechanical skills. The same variation in abilities probably applies to mathematical reasoning ability and to high-level musical skills. If the same gene(s) controlled both sides of the brain, one would expect a higher degree of correlation between types of ability than what is noted in such intelligence tests as the Wechslers.

The *Idiot Savant* Phenomenon

There is clinical evidence, too, that the patterns of growth of the two hemispheres are different. I have known since they were children two men (now middle-aged) who, as a result of the use of excessive oxygen after they were prematurely born, became totally blind (retrolental fibroplasia). In both cases, there was also a severe interruption of the development of some nerve pathways in the brain, especially those relating to language skills. Mike (not his real name) never did learn to speak, although he could understand much of what was said to him, and he didn't develop the ability to foresee risks and plan ahead for himself. Joe (another pseudonym) developed speech only to the extent of being able to parrot what was said to him and was, if anything, lower in overall functioning than Mike.

However, in spite of their blindness both developed remarkable musical skills. Mike, in particular, was a true genius on the piano, with remarkable ability to play anything he heard and to improvise in a variety of styles, from Chopin to jazz. It wasn't just imitation, either. A music teacher once visited Mike and played a composition of his own on the saxophone. He then played it a second time and Mike accompanied him appropriately on the piano.

Amazingly, he is able to generalize his musical skills. After a tragic misadventure in which he wandered out into a Minnesota blizzard and lost four fingers and part of another, he was given a marimba to play. He became remarkably skillful at that, although the last time I saw him he still preferred his piano, even with missing fingers.

The implication of this so-called *idiot savant* phenomenon is that the two halves of the brain have different schedules of growth. An event that interferes with the development of one half doesn't always affect the other. (There will be more on that subject in chapter 11). In essence, the excessive oxygen used to keep Mike alive in the neonate incubator may have caused an excessive rate of metabolism of substances needed for development of the nerve pathways genetically scheduled for the ninth month of pregnancy, which pathways were the basis for future verbal abilities. As a consequence, there would be no foundation for future development of language, which might not be expected to occur for another year or so, but it could affect future development of language abilities.

Meanwhile, the nerves related to right-brain functions, being on a separate genetic timetable, would be unaffected. In effect, the development of the two halves of the brain would involve a separate of gene or set of genes; and the two cortical areas would be genetically separate although probably close together in a physical sense.

Chapter 9

Natural and Sexual Selection

Hypothesis 6. These new abilities resulted in a tremendous evolutionary advantage, both in terms of natural selection and sexual selection. That is, not only were the individuals who expressed the gene(s) better able to survive long enough to reproduce, they also had an advantage in obtaining mates and in keeping them and their offspring alive. Consequently, in spite of a possible slight and temporary decrease in basic fertility, due to the small mismatch of the X-chromosomes with those of the aboriginal population, the carriers of the new genes increased in relative numbers.

Up to now, we have been talking about mutations. Mutations happen to individual organisms, which may or may not survive, and they may or may not pass them on to their descendants. Now we want to talk about evolution. Evolution happens to populations, and mutations are the raw material. Charles Darwin and Alfred Russel Wallace knew nothing about the physiological basis of evolution, because there was no science of genetics. In 1858, when Darwin and Wallace presented their original papers on the theory of evolution, Gregor Mendel was just getting into his experiments with peas, which led to his discovery of the basic principles of genetics; and the results were not published until 1866. Even then, Mendel's work was largely ignored until his principles were rediscovered in the early 1900s.

Nonetheless, Darwin was aware that there was some process by which individuals of any species could be changed, so as to be different from their parents; and he also knew that some of these changes could be passed on to or through their progeny. If such a change (mutation) was favorable for the individual organism in the particular situation, that individual was more likely to survive and reproduce than others of its kind. If the change was unfavorable, the individual did not survive to reproduce, or its reproduction was reduced.

Thus, a population would evolve with selection for favorable traits, and against unfavorable ones, as related to the particular environment in which it found itself. However, what are favorable traits in one situation may turn out to be unfavorable ones in another. As will be discussed in chapter 16, this applies even to such seeming universally favorable traits as intelligence in the species *Homo sapiens*.

When Darwin wrote his historic book on the origin of species, he accepted the theories of Lamarck, that mutations arise out of the needs of the organisms. This idea is still around today, and, indeed, for many years only Lamarckian genetics could be taught in the former Union of Soviet Socialist Republics (Weiss, 1991). Now we are aware that mutations arise at random. They may *seem* to arise out of needs, but when a mutation occurs that is adaptive, its bearers are the ones most likely to survive. However, for every favorable mutation there are scores of others that are maladaptive and die out.

The Difference between Natural and Sexual Selection

Darwin himself distinguished two kinds of selection. "Sexual selection depends on the success of certain individuals over others of the same sex in relation to the propagation of the species; whilst natural selection depends on the success of both sexes, at all ages, in relation to the general conditions of life." (Darwin, 1871)

Modern science has confirmed Darwin's ideas in most respects. About the only argument one might have with his definitions, as they were given in his book, *The Descent of Man and Selection in Relation to Sex* (1871), is his statement that selection depends on the success of both sexes *at all ages*. It is becoming apparent that unfavorable mutations that affect an individual, especially a human individual, after the period of reproduction and care of offspring, have no selective disadvantage. That is why many of modern medicine's greatest problems relate to the diseases of old age. Such conditions have had little or no evolutionary impact, no selection against them, since by the time they kill or disable a person, that person has already reproduced and reared a family, passing on his or her genes to another generation.

An Example of Genetic Selection

It is easier to observe the effects of natural selection in the lower forms of life than in humans. One of the classic examples was observed in England over the past century and a half, with the change in the color of some common moths, particularly *Biston betularia*. Ordinarily, up until the middle of the nineteenth century, this was a light grey moth peppered with small black dots, but basically light in color. Occasionally, though, there would be observed a melanic (opposite of albino) form that was dark in color.

What happened was that a few of these moths that carried, in addition to the usual dominant gene that determined their whitish color, a recessive gene for melanism, but they were only a little darker than the others. However, when two of these carriers of melanism mated, about a fourth of the offspring would inherit two of the genes for dark color and so would be dark gray, almost black.

Had two of these dark moths chanced to mate, all of their offspring would have been melanic, as they carried only those genes. But this didn't happen very often because their color made them particularly conspicuous against the light-colored bark of the trees on which they would rest. A bird could spot them easily, and so such a moth became a meal instead of a parent. However, the gene for melanism continued to exist in the population of moths, carried on by some of those individuals that had only one gene for it. In fact, such moths may have been more likely to survive than the others if the additional little bit of color resulting from the recessive genes for melanism made them a better match for the color of the tree bark.

Then came the industrial revolution with its soot and grime, and the bark of the trees got darker and darker. Soon the occasional melanic moths were the inconspicuous ones and the "normal" light-colored moths were easy for the birds to find. Now, a century or so later, light-colored moths are rare.

Another interesting thing happened. When black became beautiful in the moth world, additional genes that intensified the blackness became advantageous too. There could be genetic selection for these genes for blacker color, so that today's *Biston* are darker than the original melanic specimens. This selection could not take place until the genes for dark color came to the fore, although they may have existed hidden away in the genotype of the species for hundreds of thousands of years without any selective advantage at all.

The same thing probably happened with the genes for intelligence. There were in all likelihood some genes affecting speech, language or cognitive functioning that had no particular value prior to Adam. Such secondary genes could have been hidden in the pre-*Homo sapiens* genotype for tens of thousands of years before they were exposed to the processes of sexual and natural selection. That means, for one thing, that you and I are probably smarter than Adam was in an absolute sense. But not in relation to the people around us. Adam was intellectually unique in his world while you and I, bright as we may be, aren't.

Intelligence as a Positive Selection Factor

In the story of Adam and his descendants, it was pretty much taken for granted that the improved intelligence was favorable for natural selection. Adam was able to take better care of himself, to foresee situations such as food shortages, to outwit the competition for food and a place in the world, and so to survive long enough to reproduce.

In the matter of sexual selection, the fact that his descendants have taken over the world should be evidence enough. However, there also is some evidence that in a very primitive society higher levels of ability do indeed provide selective advantage.

Lessons from a Primitive People

Dr. James V. Neel (1970), in an article very appropriately entitled *Lessons from a "Primitive" People*, traced back for three generations the families of a tribe of South American Indians that had remained totally isolated from civilization. These Indians were, like our own late prehistoric ancestors (right up to Biblical times), polygynous. A male who was capable and successful could manage to have and care for several mates, while a less successful man would be lucky to have even one.

Dr. Neel found that the number of children per woman was not particularly variable. This is only to be expected because of the limitations resulting from the duration of pregnancy and the lessened fertility during the long period of nursing an infant in such societies. However, there was a great deal of variation in the numbers of descendants of the males. The polygynous men, who tended to be the more intelligent and capable ones, had large numbers of children and grandchildren. The five most prolific grandfathers had a total of 219 grandchildren, while the 50 least prolific (among those who had any grandchildren at all) had only 83. The ratio of grandchildren between the highest and lowest reproducing men was about 26 to one.

This was, and is, a very simple type of society with little differentiation by occupation—everyone is a farmer. According to the investigators, it is a remarkably egalitarian society, without hereditary titles of leadership, but rather with open competition for leadership based on innate characteristics.

Thus, the evidence from a *primitive* people is that overall ability, including intelligence, is an important factor in reproductive rate, especially of the males. The fact that Adam's gene for increased intelligence was X-linked also resulted in its being increased in frequency in the population, since the more variable sex in terms of potential reproduction was also the one to express the condition fully. To some extent, however, this was offset by the fact that at first the carrier males passed on their X-chromosome with the more favorable genes to only half of their descendants, the girls, and it could have been a couple of generations before they showed up again, at least in full force.

If the normal range of variation in intelligence or competence in the society that Dr. Neel (1970) described can result in such a great difference in reproductive rate, it is obvious that Adam and his descendants had a tremendous advantage over the persons with the primitive brain in the matter of sexual selection. It is also apparent that even up to historic times the brighter and more capable men had a continuing advantage in sexual selection. That probably applies to the women as well, but not to the same extent because of their smaller variability in reproductive rate. Dull and bright women probably bore about the same number of children over their lifetime. However, the brighter ones were better able to keep themselves alive up to and through their reproductive years and to provide their offspring with more of the means of survival.

Evolutionary Selection in the Modern World

While Dr. Neel's lesson from a primitive people has important implications as far as past evolution of increased intelligence is concerned, it should not be applied too directly to a modern, complex society. *Natural* selection, in the form of improved health and survival, both of parent and child, may still be slightly in favor of the more intelligent; but *sexual* selection now operates in the opposite direction in many parts of the world.

As Dr. Neel and his associates (Neel, Salzano, Junqueira, Kreiter, and Maybury-Lewis, 1964) pointed out in an earlier paper:

> The evidence suggests that fertility differentials have far more genetic significance in the Xavantes than for civilized people today. The position of chief or head of clan is not inherited but won on the basis of a combination of attributes (prowess in hunting and war, oratory, skill in wrestling, etc). The greater fertility of these leaders must have genetic implications. Indeed, it may be that the single most dysgenic event in the history of mankind was departure from a pattern of polygamy based on leadership, ability, and initiative.

Dr. Ernest Mayr (1970), strongly agreed with Neel's report.

> The social structure of contemporary society no longer awards superiority with reproductive success. . . . All members of the community benefit equally from the technological and other achievements of the superior individuals. Thus the below-average individual, provided he is not too far below average,

can make a living and reproduce as successfully as the above-average individual.

Intelligence as a Genetic Lethal

Indeed there are several factors that nowadays serve to make intelligence a genetic lethal, that is to result in a lower reproductive rate for persons of higher capability. Notable among these is reliable contraception. Persons of higher IQ are more likely to use contraception and to use it more consistently and effectively than persons of lower IQ.

With or without contraception, generation frequency does tend to differ between persons of different intellectual levels. In our educationally oriented society there is a tendency for the most capable persons to delay their reproduction until they have completed their education. A person with a doctorate is likely to be 30 or so before he or she gets around to the baby bit. On the other hand, many of the less capable start their families at half that age or less.

Women who start bearing their children while in their teens have more effect on the overall population than those who wait until their 20s and 30s. A woman who has her first child at the age of 15 could be having grandchildren by the time later-reproducing persons have even one child.

For another thing, there is an increasing trend for the children in larger families to be less bright than their peers. Although this trend has existed for some time, it is now apparently increasing, as Marian Van Court and Frank D. Bean (1985) pointed out. They report that over the past 50 or 75 years the tendency has been toward an increasing negative correlation between family size and intelligence. This is not solely because children in large families don't get as much attention and training as they would if they were the only child, or one of two children. There is also a definite genetic element, at least in the U. S. For instance, Van Court and Bean found a significant negative correlation between the mother's intelligence and the number of her children. On an average, then, the duller the mother, the larger the family and the duller the children. In light of the demands of modern technology for persons of higher intelligence, this is hardly a situation that one would want to encourage.

Familial Tendencies in Mental Subnormality

The matter of mentally subnormal parents having similar children has been a concern for most of the past century, and with good reason. In the early third of the century, it became obvious from clinical observation that mental subnormality ran in some families. More recently, Drs. Elizabeth and Sheldon Reed (1965) evaluated the matter scientifically and published their results in their book, *Mental Retardation: A Family Study*. One of the findings was that when both parents are mentally deficient, the risk is almost 40 percent that any child of theirs will be the same. If the mother is subnormal and the father normal, the risk is just below 20 percent; and if the father only is defective, the risk is about 8 percent. As would be expected under the hypothesis of X-linkage of major intellectual traits, the mother's genes are far more significant as a risk factor than those of the father.

Chapter 10

The Races and the Spread
of *Homo Sapiens*

Hypothesis 7. From its start in a single individual (or possibly two or more brothers), the mutant type of *Homo* spread within its original group, replacing the older type within a relatively few generations. Then, in groups and as individuals, persons carrying the new genes infiltrated other areas occupied by the older type of Man. When mixtures involving large groups occurred, racial characteristics (which were already well established) became thoroughly intermixed. When just a few individuals introduced the new genes to a population, the racial characteristics of the aboriginals remained, submerging the variable genetic characteristics of the invaders except for the improved intellect.

The Spread of *Homo Sapiens*

In his book, *The Origin of Races*, Dr. Carleton Coon (1962b, p. 657) summarizes his ideas:

> My thesis is, in essence, that at the beginning of our record, over half a million years ago, man was a single species, Homo erectus, perhaps already divided into five geographic races or subspecies. Homo erectus then evolved into Homo sapiens not once but five times, as each subspecies, living in its own territory, passed a critical threshold from a more brutal to a more sapient state.

Dr. Theodosius Dobzhansky (1970, p. 392), in *Genetics of the Evolutionary Process*, agrees that "some of these may have died out, but most races of H. erectus were eventually transformed into races of H. sapiens."

It is, of course, the thesis of *this* book that the process by which each subspecies passed to "a more sapient state" was a mutated gene on the X-chromosome, introduced by invading hordes or by intruding individuals.

In each instance, the genes for augmented intellectual growth had the same selective advantages when introduced into new populations as they did for Adam and his early descendants. The genes were undoubtedly of high adaptive value, both for natural and sexual selection (using Darwin's definitions of the terms). Being on the X-chromosome, they showed their effect in the first or second generation in males and in only a few generations in females. There were few or no pleiotropic effects that would upset other physiological systems. And, being on the X-chromosome, they did not lead to such severe problems in meiosis that the fertility of the carriers was seriously impaired.

So, by extension, the story of Adam and his first descendants is probably a reasonable description of the spread of *Homo sapiens* to all of the races of Man.

Racial Differences

This does not mean that there is no difference between races in the distribution of variants (alleles) of the genes for intellectual abilities. Because they are something we can see, we don't question the fact that there are racial differences in skin color, hair texture, facial conformation and many other characteristics. We have only to watch a few college or professional football, baseball, or basketball games to realize that there are racial differences in athletic ability. If a court ruled that professional athletic teams had to be racially balanced, with at least 75 percent Caucasian players, the quality of play in most of those sports would be decimated. Why, then, is it so difficult to believe that there are also racial differences in cognitive abilities?

The Possible Origins of Racial Differences in Abilities

Over tens of thousands of years of the evolution of *Homo sapiens* there were certainly many events that led to differential development of cognitive and other mental abilities. For instance, it is not unlikely that relatively small, closely related groups introduced the new genes to each race. In such cases there would be a *founder effect* as to the critical X-linked genes, resulting in a substantial continuing similarity of the descendants to the pioneers who were the original source of the new genes. Since the wanderers, or pioneers, who introduced their genes into the new groups were probably among the more capable persons of their time, the average intelligence of the resultant new subspecies of *Homo sapiens* would probably be higher, on an average, for the new group than for the old established subspecies. Admittedly, this is simply a guess, although the phenomenon of the founder effect is well known to experts in population genetics.

Even more important to the spread of genes for higher cognitive ability is the intensity of evolutionary selection for that trait in a given population. An environment demanding a higher degree of ability in order to survive would lead to a greater degree of selection than one more tolerant. For instance, the milder climate of southern Europe may have resulted in a less rigorous selection for certain cognitive abilities than did the colder regions of northern Europe. This is one possible explanation of the early studies that showed slightly higher average IQs for Americans of North European descent than for those of South European extraction.

The matter of evolutionary selection would be even more significant between groups living in geographically separated parts of the world, for instance, Africa and Europe. However unpopular the notion may be, especially among persons with liberal attitudes on social subjects, there is strong evidence that blacks in the United States, on average, score about one standard deviation (15 or 16 IQ points) lower than whites on most intelligence tests (see, for example, Ingle, 1968; Jensen, 1969a, 1969b; Lynn, 1991; Burnham, 1993; Herrnstein and Murray, 1994), which difference is reflected in school performance (see Reschly and Ward, 1991; Herrnstein and Murray, 1994). Further, this difference does not seem to be due entirely to cultural factors, since blacks tend to do relatively better on the verbal portions of tests (which are culture loaded) than on the performance items, which are less so (Jensen, 1971). (Note, however, that many types of "performance" items on tests are highly loaded with spatial perception factors, as will be discussed later. Such spatial factors may have arisen from a later mutation involving the nondominant half of the brain, and thus may be less well developed in persons of African origin, as discussed in chapter 11.)

American Indians, especially those who grew up on reservations, tend to be more culturally deprived than even the blacks in the United States (Kuttner, 1968, p. 707); yet they average about a half a standard deviation higher than the blacks on standard intelligence tests (Coleman, 1966). Alaskan Indians (Eskimos), severely culturally deprived as they would seem to have been, were found to do about as well as the white population on nonverbal tests (Jensen, 1969a; 1969b), possibly reflecting the rigorous selection brought about by the harsh climate.

As the "Adam" genes spread to new parts of the world different types of evolutionary pressures were involved. In Adam's tropical home, food was probably available the year around if one had the strength and physical skills to obtain it. That didn't just mean skill in hunting. In those times, Man was undoubtedly in competition with the hyena and other scavenger animals when it came to availing themselves of the leftovers of some lion's dinner, and with the monkeys and apes when it came to gathering fruit from the trees.

On the other hand, in some less-favored parts of the world, survival and reproduction would have been more likely for those specimens of *Homo sapiens* that were best able to foresee and plan for hardships such as cold winters and inconsistent food supplies. The key words there are "foresee" and "plan".

Furthermore, evolution is not just a process that existed in the distant past. It is entirely possible that an evolutionary process related to the intelligence of black persons took place in the United States and probably in some other countries as well. Numerous studies, such as those described in Bearn and Parker (1965), Reed (1969), and Baker (1981), have shown that an astonishingly high proportion of the genes in the identified black population of the United States are from non-African sources. For instance, Reed (1969) estimated that over 20 percent of the genes in American negroes are from non-African sources, a figure which is undoubtedly far too low today. With a few notable exceptions (for example, Thomas Jefferson, who had children by a black mistress) these "non-African sources" probably were not the brightest individuals in their group.

Also, as was previously mentioned, and as will be discussed in the following chapter, there is a likelihood that the genes for augmented ability at spatial perception and related logic, which can be considered an aspect of intelligence, probably arose enough later in human evolution so that it may not have been carried by those earlier traveling specimens of *Homo sapiens* who introduced the other mutation for cognitive and language functions to other parts of the world. For instance, the gene(s) could have originated in Europe and never have spread back to Africa in any great numbers.

Over all, there is no need to assume that the races of Man started out the same in cognitive ability, any more than that they started out the same in many other traits. Neither is there any reason to believe that evolutionary factors have been the same for all races. To accept these ideas is not racism, but realism. Ignoring existing differences does not help anyone; and, on the other hand, it makes it difficult, indeed almost impossible, to deal with such problems as the well-established racial differences in academic abilities and achievement. Some possible answers are discussed in subsequent chapters.

Chapter 11

Other X-linked Traits

Hypothesis 8. Because, as previously mentioned, the new mutation was unstable, further mutations at the same chromosomal location have occurred, affecting somewhat different traits. One of the most obvious and important of these paralogous genes relates to the development of the non-dominant half of the brain. While the characteristics of the so-called "right brain" are not yet well defined, they do include control of the organs of speech for the production of language. It is likely that another function is related to the ability to deal with geographical space, that is, to get around without getting lost. The mutated gene may also have increased the ability to perceive spatial relationships on a smaller scale, including what might be called mechanical ability. Other changes may include mathematical and musical abilities, and probably others not clearly defined. It is possible that this mutation actually occurred first in human evolution but did not become especially meaningful until the "Adam" mutation made it so.

The Girl with Only Half a Brain

During my earlier days in graduate school, my esteemed professor and major adviser, Dr. Starke Hathaway, provided his students with an unforgettable demonstration of the difference in function between the two halves of the brain. A very pretty 19-year-old girl had been seen by the Neurology Department of the University of Minnesota Hospitals because of a slow-growing malignant tumor that was located in the left, or dominant, hemisphere of her brain. She suffered terribly from headaches and from severe seizures, and

without treatment would soon have died. In order to eliminate the tumor
and to minimize the risk of recurrence, it was necessary to remove the entire
dominant half of her brain, with the most complete hemispherectomy that
had been done in the University Hospitals up to that time.

The operation took place right after Christmas, and about a month later
the clinical psychology students were brought in to see her. She had lost her
ability to speak meaningfully, but was beginning to understand a little of
what was said to her.

At Dr. Hathaway's direction, the class started singing "Silent Night, Holy
Night". The patient sang right along with us without missing a word. She
had lost, at least temporarily, her ability to use speech for communication,
but she still had the ability to produce speech, or singing, in a purely mechanical sense.

She had also retained her ability to get around—to locate herself in geographical space, so to speak. She could travel by city bus from her home in
south Minneapolis and could find her way around the maze of hallways in
the huge University Hospitals building without getting lost. Spatial perception, like the centers for the mechanics of speech, is localized in an area
comparable to that of cognitive and language abilities, but in the opposite
(nondominant) hemisphere of the brain. However, traits in the two halves
of the brain seem to be controlled by separate sets of genes. For instance,
many persons who are high in cognitive ability are poor in spatial perception,
and vice versa. The same seems to hold true for higher mathematical logic
(but not necessarily for the ability to do basic arithmetic computations).

I am happy to say that the last I heard of the young woman referred to
above, about 6 months later, she was learning to speak and understand
speech, though still at a childish level. It is entirely possible that she eventually regained normal functioning.

Right-Brain Mutations

As was mentioned in chapter 7, mutations involving variation in chromosome
morphology, such as the doubling of a section, tend to remain unstable for
long periods of time. And, in terms of evolutionary history, the couple of
hundred thousand years since Adam do not constitute a very long period.
During the unstable period, very likely there would be additional changes in
the area of the original doubling.

Some of these changes could result in less favorable arrangements that
would eventually be lost as the result of evolutionary selection. Others
would result in improved capabilities and would, in a primitive world, tend
to be preserved. Some of the changes might affect closely related structures.
For example, we might expect that some of the changes had affected growth

patterns of the opposite side of the brain, causing this area to have an extended period of growth, after the fashion of the original (Adam's) mutation.

Such genes, with a common background and involving parallel growth of similar functions, are known as *paralogous genes*. From clinical evidence derived from the *idiot savant* phenomenon, it seems likely that other genes at the same general site as those for spatial perception include some for higher level mathematical logic and possibly for musical ability, especially that which goes beyond performing skills.

X-Linkage and Gender Differences in Variability

One clue that leads to the belief that these characteristics, including the original "Adam" mutation, are X-linked (that is, they are located on the X-chromosome) is that males tend to show greater variability in them. For instance, it is generally accepted that males are more frequently good mechanics—that is, that they have inherited a favorable gene for spatial perception and so can see how the various parts of a device go together. At the same time, an objective observer is likely to note that the worst bumblers of all in the mechanical area are those males who just don't have that kind of ability. The males are probably neither better nor worse than the females on an average. However, they are more variable, with more who are at both the high and low ends of the scale.

This is understandable on the basis that males have only one set of genes for these X-linked characteristics, whereas females have two. If that one set is favorable, the male is likely to evidence high levels of the related abilities; if not, he does poorly. In females, on the other hand, genes for a low level of some X-linked characteristic on one X-chromosome would frequently be offset by the presence of more favorable genes on the other. And vice versa. In effect, as was pointed out by Dr. Mary Lyon (1962) a few decades ago, X-linked variable genes in females tend to be expressed as an average of the effects of each chromosome. Thus, there would be fewer females with exceptionally low levels of X-linked characteristics, and the same would be true for exceptionally high levels.

Spatial Visualization

X-linkage of genes for spatial visualization, which is related to such traits as mechanical ability, was suspected even before the localization of those genes for cognitive ability was even suspected. Dr. R. E. Stafford provided evidence of this as early as 1961. More recently, the Drs. Bock and Kolakowski

(1973) further studied the matter, using more sophisticated techniques, and came to the conclusion that about half of the X-chromosomes in the U.S. population carry a gene that leads to enhanced ability to perceive spatial relationships. In other words, the gene seems to result in an increased growth of the ability, in the same fashion as the hypothesized gene for cognitive and language abilities.

Since the recessive gene for increased development of spatial abilities is on the X-chromosome, males who have it would have the potential for higher levels of the related abilities. However, for a woman to have the enhanced abilities, she would have to have inherited the gene for the trait from *both* parents. It was the conclusion of Bock and Kolakowski (1973) that the superior gene is found on only about half of the X-chromosomes in the Caucasian population of the United States, so a female could expect to show the trait at higher levels only about a fourth of the time. A male, however, would show it whenever he inherited the gene (from his mother, of course), or about half the time.

It has long been recognized that this particular ability is closely related to mechanical and engineering ability. In fact, some of the tests of mechanical ability, such as the Minnesota Paper Form Board, are simply tests of spatial perception. That probably explains why there are more male than female engineers, mechanics, and machinists. It isn't just male chauvinism or female manipulation to get the men to do all of the dirty fix-up jobs, like changing a tire.

Since the presence of this ability at a high level would seem to be necessary for the establishment and maintenance of a high level of technology, differences between ethnic groups could be of substantial importance. Thus, evidence that there are substantial differences between racial groups on such nonverbal tests as the Raven Progressive Matrices (Jensen, 1974), which have at least the appearance of relating to spatial as well as cognitive abilities, may be especially important. Perhaps these so-called "culture-free" tests reflect abilities very important to an industrial society, even though they do not correlate well with tests of language ability.

Is it possible, then, that this gene actually arose as a new mutation in the early European population fairly late in human evolutionary history? If that should be the case, it would not have spread as widely among the peoples of some other parts of the world. This could account for the fact that the industrial revolution, which was largely based on mechanical inventions, arose and spread most rapidly in those areas of the world where the residents were of European extraction.

Another significant aspect of possible racial differences in the frequency of genes for augmented ability in spatial perception is in intelligence testing. As Jensen (1974) pointed out, one of the main arguments used to demonstrate that racial or ethnic differences in intelligence test scores are not due to environmental or educational factors is the fact that blacks (for instance) do relatively less well on the "performance" types of IQ tests than on those involving verbal learning and abilities. In effect, they actually do better on those tests that correlate with academic abilities than they do on those requiring non-verbal abilities.

Most nonverbal tests, including the Porteus Mazes, the Raven Progressive Matrices, and some of the Wechsler performance scales, to name a few, seem, on the face of them, to involve spatial perception ability. The result would be a lowering of average IQ scores for some non-Europeans on many nonverbal tests, which have been assumed to be more "culture fair" than verbal tests. That does not invalidate the tests, but it probably limits their importance for cross-cultural studies of general intelligence.

It is also tempting to speculate on whether the ability to perceive spatial relationships has something to do with reading ability. This is an area in which many times more boys than girls have disabilities. The problem could have been aggravated by the fact that boys tend to develop physically at a slower rate than girls during the early school years. The boy with marginal or slow development of spatial perception who was also slow in physical maturation (such abilities as left-to-right scanning movements of the eyes, for instance) could find himself in third or fourth grade before he had everything in order to start reading, even if he was intellectually ready. By that time, most of his classmates would be far advanced, and he would simply be labeled "dumb" and left out of the learning process.

Mathematical and Musical Abilities

Another area in which there may be X-linked growth augmentation is mathematics. Not only is there some research showing X-linkage of this trait, but there is the observation that, as would be expected of an X-linked characteristic, males are more variable in it. Although boys are 4 or 5 times as likely as girls to have serious disabilities in arithmetic, all of the great mathematicians have been male. In Bell's (1937) book, *Men of Mathematics*, 40 of the 41 persons listed in the chapter headings were male, and the one female was listed mainly because of her association with one of these males.

Sex differences in mathematical reasoning ability (as opposed to arithmetic computation) have been extensively studied. Dr. Camilla Persson Benbow, some of whose findings have been summarized in articles in the journal *Science* (Benbow and Stanley, 1980; 1981; 1983), reported on the research showing male-female differences, then summarized some of her own findings in a privately distributed paper:

After testing more than 100,000 intellectually talented 12- to 13-year-old students nationwide over a 15-year period, it is clear that there are consistent sex differences favoring males in mathematical reasoning ability. These differences are especially large at the highest levels of that ability and are found in other countries as well, even in countries where the culture is radically different than ours. The sex difference in mathematical reasoning ability can predict subsequent sex differences in achievement in mathematics and science. Thus they have some practical importance. (Personal communication, 1986)

The same disproportion may be true for the *creative* aspects of musical ability. Sex differences in creative musical ability are largely a matter of clinical reports and history; for instance, it is a historical fact that the great composers, and also the great conductors, have, without notable exception, been male.

Another bit of evidence that musical and mathematical abilities are localized on the side of the brain opposite from that for cognitive abilities is the fact that these abilities are the ones most frequently encountered in *idiots savant*. The literature is full of stories of musical and mathematical (including calendar) *idiots savant*, although there are other types as well. It is probable that at least some of these cases are due to an arrest of the development of the neurones related to cognitive and language ability at a crucial time, while the development of the other half of the brain, being on a different time schedule, was unaffected. It is even possible that, in at least some such cases, the nutritional materials needed for the developmental process could be transferred from the left brain to the right, resulting in exceptional abilities in related functions.

Chapter 12

X-linked Mental Deficiency

Hypothesis 9. Being relatively recent in evolutionary terms, the chromosomal area of the mutation has not yet become stabilized. This instability can result in occasional fresh mutations. Some of these mutations can be expected to result in mental deficits or disabilities which, being sex-linked, are more frequently manifested in males. The most damaging of such harmful remutations would probably result in the type of X-linked mental subnormality commonly called by such eponyms as Renpenning's syndrome or the Martin-Bell syndrome, which may actually be a partial or complete throwback to *Homo erectus*, modern Man's final evolutionary ancestor. In fact, continuing instability at this new (in an evolutionary sense) chromosomal locus may well be an explanation of the so-called fragile-X phenomenon which is almost invariably associated with mental subnormality, autism, or other mental disorders.

It was in the year of 1895 when Mr. G. E. Johnson presented his paper "Contribution to the Psychology and Pedagogy of Feebleminded Children" to the Association of Medical Officers of American Institutions for Idiotic and Feebleminded Persons. His introduction to the paper was:

The total number of persons living in the United States on the first day of June, 1890, and reported as feebleminded or idiotic, was 95,751, of whom 52,940 were males and 42,631 were females . . . 10,574 were colored, of whom 5,788 were males and 4,786 were females. (Johnson, 1897, p. 2)

Strangely, at least in light of later evidence, Mr. Johnson found no occasion to discuss the interesting discrepancy between the numbers of males and females with mental subnormality. There were about 24 percent more males overall. Among the "colored" the male excess was 21 percent.

Sex Ratios of Mentally Subnormal Persons

The phenomenon of greater prevalence of males among the mentally subnormal was not just restricted to a particular era. Surveys of the populations of institutions for the mentally subnormal continue to show greater numbers of males than females (table 12.1). This discrepancy persists in spite of a tendency (which probably still exists, but to a lesser degree) to institutionalize the higher functioning mentally subnormal females as a means of limiting their reproduction. That is, there has been, and still may be in some places, a practice of sterilization by institutionalization.

For instance, table 12.1 shows that in the early 1950's more mildly or moderately subnormal (moron) females were institutionalized than were males of a comparable level. However, a decided excess of males at the more severe levels of deficiency more than offset this tendency. In subsequent years, even at these milder levels of mental defect, males were more frequently placed in institutions.

Some authorities have tried to account for the excess of males in institutions with the hypothesis that males are more poorly tolerated in the home and in the community, resulting in a higher rate of institutional placement. However, community surveys of the prevalence of mental subnormality (table 12.2) generally show an even higher excess of males than do those based on institutional populations. Contrary to the impression, then, it has been the females who have been over-represented in institutional populations.

The excess of mentally subnormal males is ubiquitous. The surveys in table 12.2 include populations from Sweden to Australia, both children and adults. Many other surveys could be found by digging deeper into the literature and by seeking out government and social agency reports. Occasionally a survey *will* show less than 10 percent excess of males, but generally these fit into three categories:

1. Those involving young children, whose mental subnormality would be more frequently identified by the presence of associated physical characteristics, as in Down's Syndrome (mongolism). These disorders would, for the most part, affect the sexes about equally;
2. Those including primarily persons who are the most severely mentally handicapped. This would include those with pathological conditions involving the brain, such as genetic and chromosomal disorders, disease, and trauma, etc.; and

3. Those in which the overall frequency of psychometrically-determined subnormality is so high, due to local conditions such as an inadequate or
atypical educational system, that sex differences, although present, are
relatively small.

In that latter case, for instance, using the overall frequency of subnormality in the Imre study in table 12.2, the excess of males is reported to be
only 7 percent. But, if we also take into account that there may be some
factor operating to increase the number of persons of both sexes who are
classed as subnormal—say, a school system that does not provide traditional
education to a substantial number of the students—that could decrease the
proportion of males classified as defective or subnormal.

In that study, the adult population of "Rose" County, was reported to
have had a 7.68 percent rate of mental subnormality for males and 7.24 percent for females (Imre, 1968), a male excess of only 7 percent. However, it
probably was true that some of this high prevalence was due to the fact that
the WAIS Verbal test, which is highly dependent on a traditional academic
background, was used for ascertainment. Possibly the schools emphasized
courses other than the traditional school subjects to fit the needs of their
students, more than half of whom were black.

However, if 6 percent of the reported prevalence could be said to be due
to nontraditional schooling, with resulting lowered test scores, that would
leave 1.68 percent of the males' test scores, and 1.21 percent of the females'
scores, that were low for other reasons. At that level, the male excess would
be 39 percent, in the same range as many of the other studies in the table.

This should not be taken as an indictment of non-traditional education.
It is entirely probable that for the at least a majority of the students involved, such education was more appropriate for their individual needs. In
the types of low-level jobs they were likely to obtain, and even in their daily
life, academic skills would have only limited importance.

Overall, then, males are more frequently found in populations classified
as mentally subnormal, whether those populations are based on institutional
or community settings. The next question is whether this male excess is due
to genetic or environmental factors.

Families with X-linked Mental Subnormality

About 65 years after Mr. Johnson presented his paper, some other events
have shed some light on the causes of the excess of mentally subnormal
males. To make a good story, let us start at the point where Hanns
Renpenning, a medical student at the University of Saskatchewan, was ex-
plaining to his father his plans for the summer holiday.

Table 12.1. Residents and charges of U.S. public institutions, by sex and degree of subnormality, 1950-1962. (Minus sign means excess of females.) Adapted from Lehrke, 1978, Table 7.2.

Year	Degree of subnormality	Number of males	Number of females	M - F	% male excess (1)
1950: 63 of 96 institutions	Idiot	5,407	5,104	303	6
	Imbecile	11,097	10,385	712	7
	Moron	6,921	7,030	-109	-2
	Unclassified	1,662	1,411	251	18
1951: 57 of 95 institutions	Idiot	6,550	6,052	498	8
	Imbecile	12,610	11,849	761	6
	Moron	7,240	7,880	-640	-8
	Unclassified	1,081	807	274	35
1952: 64 of 96 institutions	Idiot	8,055	7,228	827	11
	Imbecile	14,534	13,360	1,174	9
	Moron	7,993	8,464	-471	-6
	Unclassified	1,781	1,291	490	38
1953: 69 of 98 institutions	Idiot	9,201	8,272	929	11
	Imbecile	15,753	14,457	1,296	9
	Moron	8,563	8,764	-201	-2
	Unclassified	1,735	1,331	404	30
1954: 73 of 97 institutions	Idiot	10,780	9,587	1,193	12
	Imbecile	17,705	16,298	1,407	9
	Moron	9,343	9,259	84	1
	Unclassified	3,052	2,412	640	27
1955: 77 of 99 institutions	Idiot	12,378	11,004	1,374	12
	Imbecile	20,590	18,672	1,918	10
	Moron	11,236	10,449	787	8
	Unclassified	3,601	2,729	872	32

Year / institutions	Category				
1956: 86 of 100 institutions	Idiot	14,381	12,228	2,153	18
	Imbecile	26,757	23,377	3,380	14
	Moron	14,920	13,219	1,701	13
	Unclassified	4,775	3,977	798	20
1957: 79 of 99 institutions	Idiot	14,942	12,831	2,111	16
	Imbecile	27,651	23,963	3,688	15
	Moron	15,172	13,334	1,838	14
	Unclassified	2,592	2,213	379	17
1958: 87 of 102 institutions	Idiot	17,123	14,813	2,310	16
	Imbecile	29,792	25,521	4,271	17
	Moron	16,139	13,876	3,263	24
	Unclassified	2,846	2398	448	19
1959: 86 of 106 institutions	Idiot	17,275	14,687	2,588	18
	Imbecile	29,721	25,014	4,707	19
	Moron	15,967	13,384	2,583	19
	Unclassified	2,493	2,115	378	18
1960: 78 of 108 institutions	Idiot	17,123	14,769	2,354	16
	Imbecile	31,186	25,987	5,199	20
	Moron	15,793	13,430	2,363	18
	Unclassified	2,257	1,991	266	13
1961: 81 of 113 institutions	Idiot	17,555	15,136	2,419	16
	Imbecile	31,478	26,297	5,181	19
	Moron	15,650	12,908	2,742	21
	Unclassified	2,458	2,176	282	13
1962: 91 of 124 institutions	Idiot	18,426	15,948	2,478	16
	Imbecile	32,682	26,831	5,851	22
	Moron	16,131	13,112	3,019	23
	Unclassified	2,902	2,514	388	15

1. Calculated (M-F)/F. Minus (-) sign means excess of females.

Table 12.2. Male : female ratios from some community studies of the prevalence of mental subnormality.

Reference	Population included	Number males	Number females	Male excess
Berg (1966)	Retarded persons in Denmark	11,493	8,966	28%
British Columbia Dept. of Health Service (1971)[A]	Retarded persons in British Columbia, 1970, all levels less borderline	4,699	3,471	35%
British Columbia Dept. of Health Service (1972)[A]	Retarded persons in British Columbia, 1971, all levels less borderline	4,841	3,585	35%
Hasan (1972, p. 62)	Retarded persons seen at a diagnostic center in Karachi, Pakistan	634	376	69%
Imre (1968, p. 554)[B]	Retarded persons ages 1-69 in "Rose" Co., MD	7.68%	7.21%	7%
Jensen (1971, p. 154)[B,C]	Same area as above. Adults ages 20-59 with subnormal functioning: White population- Negro population-	1.69% 21.57%	1.02% 16.49%	68% 31%
Johnson (1897)	U.S. Census for 1890: Colored population:	52,940 5,788	42,631 4,786	24% 21%
NY Dept. of Mental Hygiene (1955)	Mentally subnormal persons in Onondaga Co., NY	2,075	1,118	86%
Reed and Reed (1965)	Minnesota families over several generations	897	583	4%
Richardson and Higgins (1964)	Retarded children in Alamance Co., NC	10.0%	5.9%	69%
Scottish Council for Research in Education (1949)	Scottish children age 11 at time of test. 1932 study: 1947 study:	608 3,191	465 1,810	31% 76%
Socialstyrelsen (1972)	Residents in Swedish facilities for the retarded	9,098	6,799	34%
Sterner (1967)	Retarded children in Vasternorrland Co., Sweden	517	298	73%
Stomma and Wald (1972)	Residents of homes for low grade retarded children in Poland in 1970	4,888	3,825	28%

Table 12.2. Continued.

Reference	Population included	Number males	Number females	Male excess
Turner and Turner (1974)[A]	Retarded children, IQs 30-55, in New South Wales	1,335	1,010	32%
Verbraak (1975, p. 664)[D]	Retarded persons of all ages in the Netherlands: Severely retarded IQ <50)- Per 1000 of the same sex- Mildly handicapped (IQ to 80)- Per 1000 of the same sex-	25,618 4.07 56,505 10.6	18,263 2.93 33,972 6.4	38% 39% 66% 66%
Wunsch (1951)	Subnormal persons reported to registry in RI	3,706	2,970	25%
Total	Numerical data in table	188,833	134928	40%

A. Virtually total ascertainment.
B. See text for details of study.
C. A large study including 7,745 adults, with a very high
   level of ascertainment.
D. Highly sophisticated sampling technique, covering 4
   provinces with a population of 2.2 million, and the
   results extrapolated to the total population.

It seems that he was going to travel around the province and over into British Columbia to help investigate a family discovered by Dr. H. G. Dunn of the University of British Columbia, in which there were numerous mentally deficient males. In this family the condition was passed on as a genetic recessive, from women who were themselves mentally normal, to their sons, about half of whom ended up as mentally subnormal. Further, about half of the daughters of these women also inherited the faulty gene(s), so that they, in turn, could have mentally defective sons.

Said the senior Renpenning, "You don't have to go far afield to find such families. There are some here right in our own back yard".

So in addition to assisting in investigating and writing up for publication the family found by Dr. Dunn, Hanns enlisted the help of his professors and fellow students in tracing a family his father had pointed out. That too was written up.

The article on the original family (by Dunn, Renpenning, Gerrard, Miller, Tabata, and Federoff) was submitted to the *American Journal on Mental Deficiency*, where it appeared in May of 1963. Renpenning and his fellow workers weren't as ambitious for their article on the other family. They sub-mitted it to a smaller publication, *The Canadian Medical Association Journal*, where the time between acceptance and publication was shorter. It appeared in the November 1962 issue, months before the Dunn paper was published.

Due to the practice of naming medical syndromes after the first person to publish a description of a condition, medical student Renpenning's name, rather than that of Dr. Dunn, has been attached to the syndrome of X-linked nonspecific (that is, having no known physical or physiological basis) mental subnormality. Dr. Renpenning subsequently went on to the practice of ophthalmology in Saskatoon and stayed pretty much out of the genetics business except as it relates to diseases of the eye.

Actually, Renpenning's paper wasn't the earliest on the condition. That honor should probably go to Drs. Martin and Bell who had reported an Eng-lish family with X-linked mental subnormality back in 1943. Consequently, many experts, including Dr. John Opitz, editor of the *American Journal of Medical Genetics*, prefer to use the eponym, Martin-Bell syndrome for the condition. However, the 11 affected individuals in that study had, in addi-tion to mental deficiency, a tendency to muscle weakness that left them somewhat crippled, so possibly they were victims of a somewhat different disorder. Note, though, that several later reports, including some of mine, reported muscular weakness of a less severe degree in some affected males with X-linked mental deficiency.

Just about a year after Martin and Bell's report, Allen, Herndon and Dudley (1944) described a family in southern United States which was very similar to that of Martin and Bell. There were 24 affected males in six gen-erations of that family. In 1961, Dr. Losowsky described another English kinship, with nine affected males plus two less severely affected females. Such minimal expression of X-linked genes in females is common in sex-linked disorders.

It was a couple of years after that, shortly after the publication of the Renpenning and the Dunn papers, that I first got involved with the condi-tion. Dr. John Opitz of the University of Wisconsin at Madison visited the Cambridge (MN) State Hospital where I was working at the time, in the process of investigating still another family with 20 cases of male mental deficiency, from Wisconsin, Minnesota and North Dakota. For the pedigree of that family, see figure 12-2. The symbols used in that and subsequent pedigrees are shown in figure 12-1.

I stuck my neck out to the extent of offering to test some of the affected individuals, and later I offered to write the report for publication. Little did I know that that report would eventually turn out to be my doctoral disserta-tion, nor did I dream that I would still be studying and writing on the subject a quarter of a century later.

The dissertation included more than just the one family Dr. Opitz had first brought to my attention. As we continued working together, additional cases brought to his attention were added, so that four other families, involving 43 cases of mental subnormality, were added (figures 12-3, 12-4, 12-5 and 12-6). In two of those families there was dramatic proof of X-linkage. One of the female carriers of the defective gene (III-16 in figure 12-2) had similarly affected sons by two husbands; and another (II-4 in figure 12-6) had three such sons by three different husbands. By her third husband, that lady also had two daughters, each of whom had a 50 percent risk of being a carrier of the syndrome.

At first I supposed that Renpenning's syndrome was something relatively rare. However, as I started working with schools, social agencies, and institutions for the mentally deficient after my graduation, I found out that the condition was not at all unusual. It got so that I didn't even consider it worthwhile to take notes on the examples I found in schools, through welfare agencies, and through observations in the community.

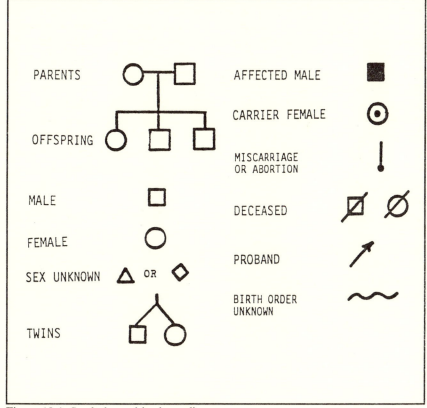

Figure 12-1. Symbols used in the pedigrees.

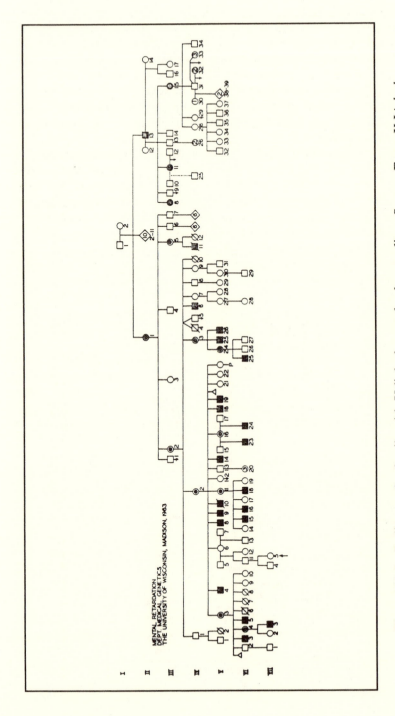

Figure 12-2. Pedigree of a family with X-linked mental subnormality. *Source:* From *X-Linked Mental Retardation and Verbal Disability*, by Robert Lehrke. 1974. March of Dimes Birth Defects Foundation. Reprinted by permission of the publisher.

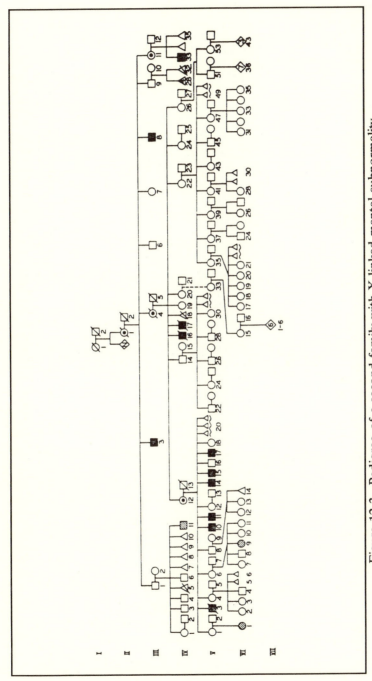

Figure 12-3. Pedigree of a second family with X-linked mental subnormality. From Lehrke (1968), Figure 9.

91

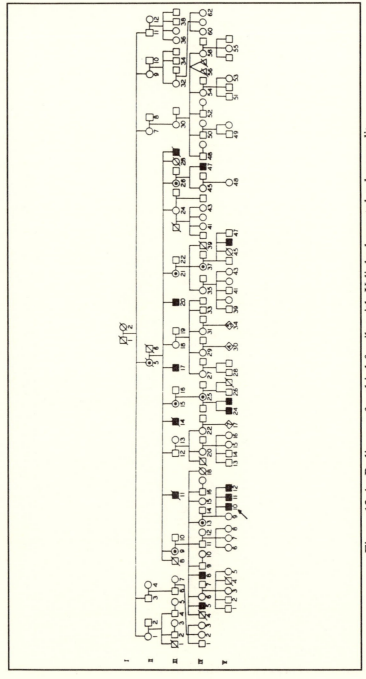

Figure 12-4. Pedigree of a third family with X-linked mental subnormality. From Lehrke (1968), Figure 10.

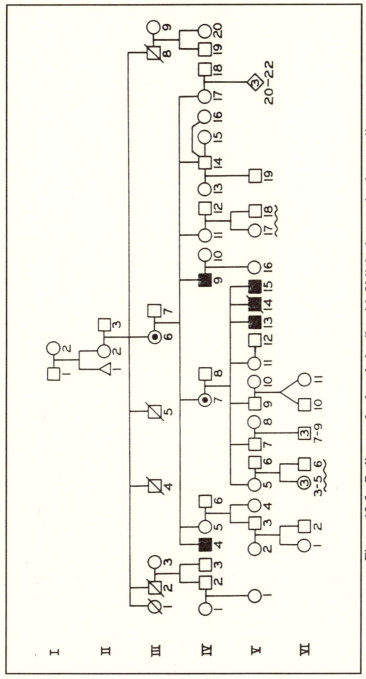

Figure 12-5. Pedigree of a fourth family with X-linked mental subnormality. From Lehrke (1968), Figure 11.

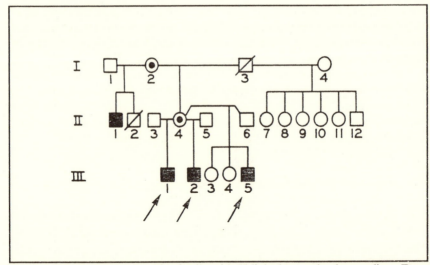

Figure 12-6. Pedigree of a fifth family with X-linked mental subnormality. From Lehrke (1968), Figure 12.

It became apparent that the reason the condition was so little known was not that it was rare but because of the practical difficulties involved in diagnosing it. Had there been physical signs, such as those found in Down's syndrome (mongolism), phenylketonuria (PKU), or the mucopolysaccharidoses (gargoylism), for example, the condition could be diagnosed from a single case. It wasn't until Lubs (1969) discovered that in some cases of X-linked mental retardation there was a tendency for the X-chromosome to break up when cultured in a nutrient-deficient medium that there was, *but just in those cases*, a means of diagnosing the syndrome from a single case. (There will be more on the subject of the fragile-X syndrome later in this chapter.)

Verbal Disability in Affected Individuals

A characteristic of those families that I studied in which adequate psychological testing was available was a tendency to verbal or cognitive disability that was far more marked than for other areas. (This was previously discussed in chapter 8). The Wechsler intelligence tests, such as the Wechsler Intelligence Scale for Children (WISC) and the Wechsler Adult Intelligence Scale (WAIS), do provide separate scales for verbal and nonverbal abilities, but because their standardization only goes down to the 40s in IQ, they cannot be used with the more severe cases of Renpenning's syndrome.

In the first family I studied, however, it happened that 11 of the 20 mentally subnormal boys and men were bright enough to take one of the

Wechsler tests, and in every such case the verbal IQ was much lower than the performance IQ. In fact, in several cases the performance IQ was well up into the normal range. Test data for the affected members of this family are given in table 12.4.

Even in cases where the person's IQ was too low to measure by means of the Wechsler tests, there was almost always some comment by the psychological examiner regarding the subject's verbal or language limitations. Dunn's report on the British Columbia family, previously mentioned, also referred to verbal disability as a characteristic of the affected males.

Consistency of Effects of the Gene Within Families

Moreover, the gene seemed to have a remarkably consistent effect on IQ within a single family, where the environmental background can be assumed to be fairly similar. The differences between affected persons within an extended family was generally much greater than it was between sets of affected brothers. Table 12.3 gives comparisons between brothers who happened to be administered the same intelligence test. (Due to differences in standardization and in statistical characteristics, IQs from different tests are not comparable).

For example, two of the brothers in the first family studied (figure 12-2) had IQs of 33 and 34 respectively on the Binet. Two other brothers in the same kinship had verbal IQs of 56 and 58 on the Wechsler Intelligence Scale for Children. Of seven brothers, four who took the Wechsler Adult Intelligence Scale (WAIS) had verbal IQs of 57, 58, 61 and 61. The three who took the Stanford-Binet showed more variation, with IQs of 47, 52, and 62; but because of the characteristics of the test, which uses different test items at different age levels, this is not a great deal of variation for tests given at different age levels of the subjects (see table 12.3).

If it is assumed that the X-linked gene for intellectual development remains the same between families and over generations of a kinship (which isn't at all certain), the variation between sibships within an extended family presumably reflects differences in environments and interacting genes. However, the X-linked gene is the primary determiner of the level of functioning. Those having the defective gene are retarded or very dull when it comes to verbal and cognitive skills.

The higher nonverbal (performance) IQs seemed to be reflected in higher levels of capability when it came to practical living skills. Ezra M., for instance, was a dignified older gentleman who had never done well in school and who had been cared for by relatives for most of his life. When I met him, though, he was living semi-independently, doing his own shopping, and even making valid price comparisons as he did so. His nephew, Erwin C.,

Table 12.3. IQs of brothers with Renpenning's Syndrome, within an extended family. Identification numbers refer to figure 12-2.

Carrier (mother)	Affected Male	Test used	IQ
II-2	III-4	Binet	52
	III-9	Binet	47
	III-10	Binet	62
	III-8	WAIS Verbal	61
	III-14	WAIS Verbal	58
	III-18	WAIS Verbal	57
	III-19	WAIS Verbal	61
II-3	III-25	Binet	33
	III-26	Binet	34
III-11	IV-15	WISC Verbal	56
	IV-16	WISC Verbal	58

whose Binet IQ was 34 and whose speech was also decidedly defective, was nonetheless capable of being left in charge of the milking and other chores on a small farm. Erwin's brother, Lester, whose IQ was 33, and whose speech was almost as defective as his brother's, managed to find his way around a 40-mile complex of country roads while hitchhiking home from the institution from which he had escaped, but he could understand only the simplest of verbal directions. (The names, of course, are pseudonyms.)

The Prevalence of X-linked Mental Subnormality

Just because this chapter has emphasized mental subnormality among males, it should not be assumed that females do not also show the effects of the gene. Generally this will be to a lesser extent (for reasons that will be further discussed in chapter 13), but in some cases an affected male could mate with a woman who is a carrier. In such cases, about half of the daughters would inherit a faulty gene from both parents and, with no offsetting "normal" gene, could be mentally subnormal.

There is also reason to believe that the faulty gene is not completely recessive to the normal one. Thus it would be possible for a female to be dull or mildly subnormal if she has inherited the faulty gene from either parent, even though the homologous gene may be completely satisfactory. Still she would not be as severely affected as a male with the same defective gene, for example, a brother.

Such milder expression in females has actually been observed. The Drs. Turner, who worked in Australia, suspected that this was the case in some of the families they studied (personal communication, 1972); and one of the earliest studies of the phenomenon of X-linked mental subnormality, that of Losowsky in 1961, included two cases of mildly affected females.

Because of this partial expression in females, then, it cannot be said that the noted excess of males with mental subnormality tells the whole story regarding the deleterious effects of the faulty X-linked genes. There are also females who are retarded or of borderline intelligence due to the effects of the gene.

In one of the major works on the subject, Dr. John Opitz (1986, p. 7) confirmed an earlier estimate of mine regarding the prevalence of X-linked mental subnormality, originally published in Lehrke (1968) and Lehrke (1978). The original computation was based on the assumption that there are 50 percent more affected males than females, which is probably excessive for severe subnormality, but conservative when mild and borderline cases are included.

To quote Dr. Opitz, "Thus, Lehrke's conclusion that '0.2 (20%) of all mental retardation (33.33% of that in males) is X-linked'. . . . appears fully substantiated." In fact, he goes on to point out that this estimate may have been conservative.

The estimate Dr. Opitz quoted is one based on the assumption that there are numerous sites on the X-chromosome, that is, numerous genes, related to intellectual functioning. That would mean that very few females would inherit two of the same faulty genes and thus be subnormal. However, later evidence would seem to indicate that only one major genetic site is involved, in which case another estimate would be more appropriate.

As the original works (Lehrke, 1968; Lehrke, 1978) pointed out, with only one chromosomal site involved, there would also be substantial numbers of females who would be homozygous for the gene and consequently would be affected. In that case, the estimate would be that 28 percent of all cases with clinical levels of mental subnormality would be males with the disorder, and an additional 8 percent would be females with the disorder. *On this basis, 36 percent of all mental subnormality—47 percent of that in males and 20 percent of that in females—would be X-linked* (Lehrke, 1974).

And if we subsume under the term "mentally subnormal" persons classified as "borderline" (IQs in the approximate range of 70 to 85), X-linked genes would turn out to be the cause of mental subnormality in a substantial majority of all cases, perhaps as much as 90 percent. This does not include those cases of learning disorders due to defective "right-brain" functions, such as reading and arithmetic disabilities which will be discussed later.

A Scientific Dilemma

At least for the moment we'll ignore the societal and financial costs of those cases of mental subnormality that are due to X-linked factors, except to admit that they are huge, and go on to the problem that the condition poses for scientists. X-linked mental deficiency, while undoubtedly an inherited disorder, simply doesn't fit into the established patterns of such disorders.

As Opitz (1986) pointed out, the syndrome of nonspecific X-linked mental retardation occurs with such a high frequency that under the Hardy-Weinberg law, an unusually high mutation rate would be needed to keep up with the attrition due to the reduced reproductive fitness of the affected individuals. (The Hardy-Weinberg law is an axiom of population genetics, with the implication that genetic conditions that limit reproduction of the victims would eventually disappear if new mutations of the same type didn't keep occurring). And it isn't just the affected males that have reduced reproductive rates. Some mothers and sisters of the mentally subnormal males also limit their families when they become aware of the genetic risks. In spite of this, the frequency of cases of X-linked mental subnormality continues to be high and is probably even increasing. As Opitz (1986, p. 8) put it:

> The conclusion is almost forced on one, namely that the MBS [Martin-Bell Syndrome, one name for the classic form of X-linked mental subnormality] is not due to a conventional Mendelian gene mutation, but rather represents a most unusual genetic condition, one perhaps prototypic of a whole new class of disorders intermediate between Mendelian and aneuploidy syndromes.

That would be an accurate description of the situation if we accept the "Adam" hypothesis. The original mutation would indeed have been an aneuploidy, that is an unbalanced event involving the physical characteristics of a chromosome. Over thousands of generations, Mendelian selection has made the mutated X-chromosome the norm.

However, since it is a very new mutation in evolutionary terms, it has not reached a point where it is stable in its form. Rather, it is subject to relatively frequent remutations, many of which undoubtedly result in mental defect. These can be passed on as Mendelian characteristics, and be subject to Mendelian selection.

Being X-linked, with the female carriers usually showing little effect of the mutation, the critical genes would continue to be passed on for many generations, even in the unlikely event that males with X-linked mental retardation would never reproduce. However, according to the Hardy-Weinberg law, for each affected male who did not reproduce, one X-chromosome carrying the critical gene would be lost to posterity, so that over a number of generations the gene would be eliminated if new mutations didn't occur. The presumption is that new mutations do continue at a great frequency.

If X-linked mental subnormality is indeed a continuing secondary manifestation of the "Adam" mutation, the remutation should occur in all of the races of Man. Table 12.2 suggests that is indeed the case. In every part of the world where the prevalence of mental subnormality has been counted, more males than females are mentally deficient.

The Fragile-X Syndrome

Beginning in the late 1960s, persons studying chromosome cultures of individuals affected with X-linked mental subnormality often encountered an unusual phenomenon. The X-chromosome sometimes shattered into two or more pieces.

Later on, when using an improved culture medium, the phenomenon did not show up; but when the researchers returned to the earlier type of medium, which actually was deficient in folic acid, an essential nutrient, they again encountered breakage of the X-chromosome in many cases. In fact, they labeled the condition "the fragile-X syndrome" and considered it to be a second form of X-linked mental deficiency, distinct from those cases in which the breakage did not occur, which they continued to call by the eponyms "Martin-Bell syndrome" or "Renpenning's syndrome" as before. More recently, many authorities call all cases of non-specific X-linked mental subnormality "fragile-X", regardless of the chromosomal findings, or lack thereof. In fact, they found the fragile chromosomes in less than 60 percent of the cells in most affected individuals (American College of Medical Genetics, 1996).

Not only was the cytogenetic test for fragile-X unreliable, it was costly and slow. However, in the early 1990s the actual gene for the condition was identified. It was found that this so-called FMR1 gene could be identified by an increased number of nucleotides at a critical site on the X-chromosome. While the number of CCG (cytosine-cytosine-guanine) nucleotides at that chromosomal location in the normal population varies from 6 to approximately 50, some affected individuals had more than 200 repeats. The severity of the fragile-X syndrome seems to be a function of the number of insertions (Travis, 1995), possibly varying as the number differed from some optimal configuration.

There is no clear line of demarcation between the normal and abnormal individuals. In the middle range, from 45 to 55 repeats, there is a "grey zone" where diagnosis is uncertain. While the new test based on these findings is still less than perfect, it is much more reliable and far less expensive than the older method (American College of Medical Genetics, 1996). In light of present knowledge, it is likely that all X-linked forms of otherwise-unidentified mental deficit—subnormality, developmental delay and some types of autism—should be considered as candidates for the cytogenetic test, along with possible carriers. That is not to say that knowledge of the diagnosis can lead to effective treatment. However, with suitable counselling, there can be an understanding of the genetic implications which could enable families to utilize appropriate family planning.

The breakage of X-chromosomes in nutrient-deficient culture media could be due to differences in the size of the normal and abnormal gene at the FMR1 locus. Such irregularities would lead to erratic pairing during meiosis, which could result in abnormalities leading to varying degrees of chromosome breakage under stressful conditions of mitosis. In effect, the fragile-X condition would be a variable *trait* rather than a distinct *type*, and a secondary symptom rather than a cause of the basic disorder. This probability is increased by the recent discovery that the FMR-1 gene, which is the site of the primary break, is sometimes "silent" in that it does not result in chromosome breakage in some known carriers of the gene (Bishop, 1991).

New Discoveries

A possible explanation is that the "Adam" mutation arose as the result of a change in the number of neucleotides at the critical site, a "molecular disease" that had positive consequences. The condition that was an abnormality in Adam's time was so beneficial that over the centuries it has become the norm. Now, a reversion to the "Adam" conformation is harmful.

Thus, while fragility, per se, of the X-chromosome is frequently associated with X-linked mental subnormality (Opitz, 1986), it is not the cause. The assumption of *Post hoc, ergo propter hoc* [After this, therefore because of this] again turns out to be false. It is much more probable that both the fragile chromosome and the mental problem have a common causality, a change in the physical characteristics of a section of the X-chromosome. This would affect not only the expression of certain genes but also the matching up of chromosomes during meiosis, the process by which new chromosomes are formed. Physical differences in the size of the parental X-chromosomes during the matching-up process in the previous generation could create loops, which are known to be unstable, and thus accounting for the fragility.

Favorable X-Linked Mutations and Fragile-X

Favorable mutations at the site could also be expected. These could result in the occasional male genius born to relatively mediocre parents or the girl who turns out to be significantly brighter than would be expected from her genetic background. It would be interesting to learn whether the number of nucleotide repeats at the locus are below average among such people. Could it be, for instance, that chromosome studies would in time replace intelligence tests?

The Significance of X-linked Factors to Mental Subnormality

Perhaps the best way to understand the significance of X-linked factors to mental subnormality is to go over the material on categories of mental retardation (to revert to the popular term) in most modern textbooks on the subject. The following material, however, is not taken from such a textbook, but from a lecture given by Dr. Arthur R. Jensen before the Fourth International Congress of Human Genetics in Paris, France, on September 9, 1971.

To quote Dr. Jensen (with his permission):

> Two broad categories of mental deficiency are now generally recognized. The first is comprised of those conditions resulting from (a) chromosomal anomalies (e.g., Down's Syndrome or "Mongolism"); (b) major gene defects whereby a single mutant gene, usually recessive, completely overrides the normal determinants of mental development (e.g., phenylketonuria and microcephaly); (c) brain damage due to infectious disease or trauma (e.g., maternal rubella, encephalitis, eclampsia). The vast majority of the most severely retarded, with IQs below 50, belong in this category.

> The second category consists of what is now called familial mental retardation. The vast majority of these individuals are mildly retarded, with IQs between 50 and 70. (The upper limit seems quite arbitrary and has been placed anywhere from 70 to 85). At least 80 to 90 percent of persons in this IQ range appear clinically normal and show no history or signs of neurological damage.

> The first category of retardation, although it is continuous with the normal distribution of intelligence in the population, is in a sense separate from it. It is superimposed upon the normal distribution and creates the "bulge" at the lower tail of the distribution, that is, the excess over the frequency of low IQs that would be expected from a poly-genic and microenvironmental model of the distribution of intelligence in the population.

> The second category of retardation, that is, the so-called familial variety, on the other hand, can be viewed as just the lower tail (about 3 percent) of the normal distribution. Although such retardation constitutes normal variation rather than a pathological condition, for the individual it is usually a severe handicap educationally, occupationally, and socially. Such persons as adults in a modern industrial society can seldom manage on their own and they usually require various social services for their welfare.

Dr. Jensen refers to the normal curve and the "bulge" superimposed thereon by conditions, essentially single events, that cause physiological damage to the brain and thereby decrease its level of functioning. The area under the normal curve is the expected distribution of IQs in the population, with the exception of such single events. *In effect, barring events resulting in physiological damage to the brain or nervous system, an individual's intellectual position relative to the normal curve would be a function of his or her X-linked genes for intelligence; to a lesser degree the quality of his or her environment; and, to a minor extent, interactions between intelligence and environment. Thus, X-linked intellectual deficits would be the "familial" aspect of cultural-familial mental retardation.*

Figure 12-7 shows the theoretical and presumed actual distributions of IQs for the total population. Under the X-linkage hypothesis, however, there would be somewhat different distributions for males and females. This is discussed further in chapter 13.

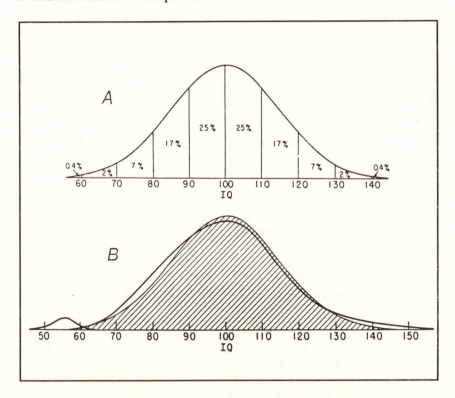

Figure 12-7. **A**. Theoretical distribution of IQs in the population. **B**. Comparison of the theoretical (shaded area) and actual distributions. The hump at the lower end is exaggerated for clarity.

The Etiology of X-Linked Mental Subnormality

There are many types of X-linked physical or physiological disorders result-ing in mental deficiency, including Hunter's syndrome, the Lesch-Nyhan syn-drome, and at least one form of hydrocephaly. In each of these syndromes there is an identifiable abnormality that results in physical damage to the brain and consequent intellectual subnormality. These conditions, however, account for only a small part of the noted excess of males with intellectual deficit. The rest of the cases must be due to some X-linked condition that is not a physical or physiological disorder with primary or secondary effects on the brain, but rather a flaw in the development of intelligence, per se.

The implication of the Lehrke hypothesis is that the cause of these disor-ders is a remutation of the chromosomal areas controlling the growth pat-terns of certain nervous pathways. As such, they affect the genes for the de-velopment of intelligence specifically. They do not, as in other forms of genetically transmitted mental subnormality, cause a physiological aberration that leads to damage to the brain, and thus secondarily affect intellectual capabilities.

Furthermore, the remutation within a kinship has a remarkably consistent effect on intellectual functioning, not only within sibships but over genera-tions within a family (see table 12.3.) However, these remutations vary sub-stantially between pedigrees (Lehrke, 1968, 1974), so the evidence suggests that there are many of them.

X-Linkage of the Basis for Cultural-Familial Mental Subnormality

This introduces the factor of variability into the picture. It is highly likely that X-linked remutations constitute a major portion of the entire range of the "familial" aspect of cultural-familial mental deficiency. In effect, it is questionable whether sets of genes resulting in what is today considered to be mental subnormality have been passed on over thousands of generations from a mating of a person carrying the "Adam" gene with with some individ-ual of the *Homo erectus* subspecies. As Neel, Salzano, Junqueira, Kreiter, and Maybury-Lewis (1964) pointed out (see chapter 9), intelligence was probably a far greater *positive* selective force in primitive societies than it is in the modern world, when it may have become a negative selection factor.

It is also probable that in those areas of the world where survival was most difficult, the selection for higher intellect was strongest. In effect, the harsher the climate and the greater the deprivation, the greater the selection for cognitive and planning ability. This could account for at least some of the racial differences described in publications such as *The Bell Curve* (Herrnstein and Murray, 1994).

Verbal vs. Nonverbal IQs in Renpenning Syndrome

An important aspect of the Renpenning type of X-linked subnormality is that it affects verbal skills more than nonverbal. Table 12.4 compares the Wechsler verbal and performance IQs of the affected males in one of the families studied. The performance IQ averaged 12.8 IQ points higher.

Deficits of Right-Brain Functions

This does not mean that there are not cases in which the Performance IQ is depressed on a familial basis. Such cases may actually be more frequent than the other type. However, as they do not show up as markedly in school performance and socioeconomic functioning, except possibly relative to reading and arithmetic disabilities, the situation is not recognized.

It should be recalled that spatial perception, probably a component of certain of the performance subtests of the Wechsler tests, is also apparently X-linked. In fact, disability in the area of spatial perception may be a major factor in boys' reading and arithmetic disabilities due to their inability to recognize the shapes of letters and numbers and to distinguish right from left. Disorders of mathematical *reasoning* are probably also X-linked. Such right-brain deficits could account for the frequency of learning disorders involving reading and arithmetic in boys, to be discussed in the next chapter.

Prevalence of X-Linked Mental Subnormality

In the dissertation containing the original exposition of the theory of X-linkage of major intellectual traits (Lehrke, 1968) and subsequent publications, it was estimated that, at a minimum, 20 percent of all mental subnormality at clinical levels (33 percent of that in males) would be X-linked. This was based on the assumption that numerous genetic loci were involved, which was the prevailing view at the time.

However, the original source also pointed out that if only one locus is involved, as now seems likely, that estimate rises to 36 percent of all cases of mental subnormality—47 percent of those in males and 20 percent of those in females. In either case, the number of cases of X-linked mental defect far exceeds that for Down's syndrome (mongolism), which once was thought to be the most prevalent type of mental deficiency.

The clinical level of X-linked mental defect (say, IQs below 60) then blends imperceptibly into milder levels, where it becomes identified as cultural-familial mental subnormality. In other words, the "familial" aspect of cultural-familial mental deficiency is X-linked.

Table 12.4. Wechsler intelligence test data on some mentally subnormal members of the family shown in figure 12-2. Adapted from table 18 in Lehrke (1968).

ID No.	Test	Full Scale IQ	Verbal IQ	Performance IQ	(P-V IQ)
II-6	WAIS	67	64	75	11
III-8	WAIS	69	61	81	20
III-14	WAIS	66	58	81	23
III-18	WAIS	58	57	64	7
III-19	WAIS	59	61	63	2
IV-3	WAIS	85	79	95	16
IV-5	W-BI	81	76	91	15
IV-15	WISC	56	56	65	9
IV-16	WISC	59	58	68	10
IV-23	WISC	73	69	83	14
IV-25	WISC	83	78	92	14
Mean Median		68.7 67	65.3 61	78.0 81	12.8 14

From there, the milder cases come to be classified as "borderline". Again, X-linkage is apparent, mainly because more males are affected.

When it comes down to a final analysis, then, almost all mental deficiency that is not specifically due to physical or physiological damage to the central nervous system is X-linked. There are various degrees of the same disorder, with some differences, such as fragile X-chromosomes, in secondary symptoms. Undoubtedly, due to Darwinian selection, the more severe forms are the result of more recent mutations than the less severe. The more severe the mental defect, the more rapidly the mutation would be removed from the gene pool. However, as was mentioned in chapter 9, borderline levels of mental subnormality may be a positive selection factor in many parts of the modern world due to increased levels of reproduction of the carriers—sexual selection of the marginally fit.

Until the syndrome of X-linked mental subnormality becomes better known to physicians, psychologists and mental health professionals in general, the condition will continue to present a diagnostic problem, since it cannot be readily identified from a single case, as can those involving metabolic or chromosome disorders. However, when there is wider knowledge that the condition exists and is fairly common, diagnosticians will learn to look at the family tree for the pattern of sex linkage. In addition, there are now laboratory tests that can be used (Travis, 1995) whenever the family history is inconclusive.

For the present, even when there are several cases in an extended family, the pattern of genetic sex-linkage is not well enough known for it to suggest a hereditary basis for the condition. The usual method of dealing with cases of unidentified mental subnormality is for the affected boys (and occasionally, girls) to be examined by a school psychologist, or sometimes by the family physician, leading to a recommendation for special class placement, but with no mention that there is a risk for additional cases among children of the mothers, maternal aunts, sisters, and female cousins on the maternal side. As a consequence, the genetic basis for what is now recognized as by far the most common form of intellectual deficit goes undetected.

Even when the genetic nature of the problem is discovered, religious or social pressures may interfere with efforts to avoid further cases. While working at one of Minnesota's institutions I ran across a family whose first child was normal, but whose seven other children were all afflicted with increasing levels of mental deficit and spasticity. Four of these were institutionalized, the other three remained at home, but had been in special classes for the "learning disabled". The condition was due to kernicterus, Rh incompatibility, not to X-linked genes, but the implications are the same, except that in this case the retardation and spasticity would be even more severe in each subsequent child; and it would be impossible for that couple to have a normal child.

I brought up the situation at weekly rounds and it was decided that an experienced social worker would visit the family and explain the situation, in hopes of preventing any further severely handicapped children. After all, the seven disabled children were already a severe expense to the State.

When the social worker reached the home in northern Minnesota, she found that the Catholic chaplain (who also participated in rounds) had already been there and urged the family, which was Roman Catholic, to ignore what the social worker had to say, since the retardation "was God's will." I don't know what the family's decision was in the matter, but I do know that within a few days the chaplain was transferred to a tiny rural parish.

The replacement chaplain was a Benedictine monk who had spent his career in a monastery setting. I had been a bit concerned about his feelings toward me, and toward my interest in preventing retardation, but not for long. One day he came to me, while I was having coffee in the staff dining room, for a private talk.

His attitude was that the matter had been a decision by the professional staff of the hospital, who represented the State, and that his predecessor had

had no business interfering with such a decision. "Render unto Caesar the things that are Caesar's," was his rationale.

Unfortunately, in all too many cases, decisions about birth control and sterilization of those mentally subnormal persons who are receiving government or privately financed services are subject to the regulations of the organization providing such services. For instance, a mildly retarded woman had been placed in a state institution, mainly to control her fertility, since she had already had two children that she was unable to care for adequately. Although she was legally married, the husband was uninterested in the children (at least one of whom was his) and unwilling or unable to be of much help, so the children had to be cared for by her mother.

To complicate matters, the woman (with reason) hated the institution where she had been placed and her loss of freedom, and on several occasions she managed to run away. Twice, on such elopements, she became pregnant. For instance, a truck driver, who picked her up while she was hitch hiking on a cold winter night, kindly shared his hotel room.

Under a more humane administration of the institution, it was decided that her fertility wasn't a crime that deserved long-term incarceration and she was returned to the care of her family. From a common-sense point of view, it certainly would have been wise to do a tubal ligation, but that was not possible since she was deemed legally incompetent to consent to her own sterilization! In fact, it wasn't even permissable for the institution's physician to provide her with a prescription for contraception. The medical administrator went out on a limb so far as to ask the woman's parents to stop off on their way home so that a physician in the community could fit her with a diaphragm, hardly a reliable method for a dull, irresponsible, and very fertile woman! (That was in the days before the birth control pill, which may not have been much better in that particular case.)

Nowadays, of course, there are implants for longer term contraception, and modern techniques of sterilization that are far less risky and traumatic than the hysterectomies and tubal ligations of the past. The major problems with their use are religious, philosophical and, all too often, legal.

Chapter 13

X-linkage and Learning Disorders

Hypothesis 10. The hypothesis that the effects of the X-linked genes, normal or abnormal, show up in the growth patterns of certain areas of the brain can be used to explain many previously puzzling aspects of mental retardation and learning disorders. In cases where an allele (variant) of the X-linked genes results in a relatively slower onset or development of the neuronal connections involved in cognitive development and/or spatial perception, there could be difficulty for the affected individual in adapting to the rigid, age-specific demands of school and society—mental *retardation* in a literal sense. When the delay involves only a limited area, the condition is more likely to be considered a learning disorder. In at least a few cases, such a slower start could be offset by a longer or more rapid period of growth before leveling off. That pattern, which would be more often apparent in males, could explain many cases of school failure in persons who, as adults, turn out to be in the normal range of intelligence—normal but under-educated. *In effect, due to X-linkage there would be expected to be greater male variability in the age of readiness for basic education.* Furthermore, if it should be the case that such slower maturation is more frequent among children of certain ethnic groups (both boys and girls would be affected), that could be of great significance in planning educational programs for them.

Five months after conception, long before it is ready to meet the outside world, the human fetus has all of the 100 billion or so neurones that will make up the core of its nervous system (that is, U.S. billions, 10^9, not British billions, 10^{12}). What it lacks is the complex network of interconnections that make life and intelligence possible.

In the next two or three months, enough of the interconnections have been made so that the infant could possibly survive if brought into the world prematurely. By 9 months after conception, at the normal time for birth, enough connections exist so that vital functions such as sucking (nursing) and breathing can take place and the child is able to cry in response to discomfort. There are random, but somewhat coordinated, movements of the body, some protective reflexes, and a certain amount of sensory input.

These connections do not grow at a rate that is consistent among different parts of the brain, but rather each area has its own schedule. For instance, somewhere in the final month or so of a normal gestation period there occurs an important preliminary development of the interconnections in that part of the brain that will later be involved in speech and in the more advanced aspects of intelligence. In many cases, disturbance of that development by something such as disease, insufficient oxygen, or even the use of excessive oxygen with premature babies (which can also cause blindness), can result in serious disruption of cognitive and language skills later on, even though other mental functions may be normal or even above average. This may be the explanation of at least some cases of *idiots savant* (the condition in which some mentally deficient persons have normal or even exceptional ability at mathematics, music, or the like) and of the type of mental subnormality called *autism*. In these disorders, the ability to use language for communication and for complex thought is damaged while the other abilities develop normally or even better than average.

The Growth of Intellectual Abilities

In the absence of such disruptive events, though, the growth of mental abilities continues on a variable timetable, but in a highly predictable sequence, up until the teens or early adult years. By the age of a year to 18 months, the average child is able to associate meaning with some sounds he or she hears, and to recognize that certain of the sounds he or she randomly produces lead to rewarding situations. For instance, the sounds "mama" will bring pleasant attention when the mother is around. In another 6 months, the child will be making many more vocalizations, many of them imitations of words that are meaningful to others, but more as a matter of play than for communication. By the age of 3 or 4, the child will be using words to identify objects or events in the immediate environment. It is a reasonable conjecture that at about this level the language abilities of *Homo erectus* leveled off.

It is not until the seventh or eighth year that the average child has much capability of thinking and speaking in abstract terms. The average child of 6 may or may not be able to explain the difference between a bird and a dog. Oh, he or she knows what a dog is, and what a bird is, all right. The child just isn't sure what a "difference" is. The point is that "bird" and "dog" are concrete concepts, while "difference" is abstract. The ability to understand and use abstract concepts comes later in life than for concrete ones, and some people never do reach the stage of abstract thinking. The ability to use foresight (independently, not as a learned action) begins at about the same time as that for abstract thought.

A limited ability to plan ahead probably characterized our early caveman ancestors. While an adult *Homo sapiens* would be able to foresee the need for fire as he starts on a long trip, and so carry a smoldering stick along with him, his *Homo erectus* antecedent would be more likely to have to do without. It is not just a coincidence that the name, Prometheus, for the god who, in Greek mythology, was reported to have brought the gift of fire to mankind, translates to "foresight".

Patterns of Mental Growth

In observing a child's growth, it is not hard to see how physical abilities and motor coordination increase with age. The peewee leaguer doesn't have the ability of the high school athlete, no matter how thoroughly he may have been coached. But unless one is acquainted with the use of intelligence tests, it is much harder to see the increase of mental abilities (as differentiated from learning) over the years. Like physical abilities, cognitive abilities do grow with time, up to a point that is mainly determined by one's genetic makeup. Then they level off, usually sometime in the teens or early twenties. This pattern, of course, applies to cognitive capabilities, not to learning or knowledge. We continue to learn until severe senility hits us. The forgetfulness of old age is not so much due to forgetting, per se, as to the inability to notice or encode, to actually learn, in the first place. Note that facts already learned, even many decades in the past, are *not* forgotten (although they may be distorted) except in the more extreme cases of senility such as Alzheimer's disease.

Figure 13-1 is a theoretical display of what is generally accepted to be typical growth patterns at different levels of IQ. For many reasons, these patterns can only be considered approximate, and any individual is likely to vary from the theoretical. Note that there is a tendency for those persons whose rate of mental growth is the fastest to continue such growth for a longer period. That is, bright persons get brighter both faster and for a longer period than the less bright.

It is the thesis of this book that the genes controlling the growth of interconnections (axones and/or dendrites) between nerve cells within the brain, and thus the pattern of mental growth, are on the X-chromosome; and also

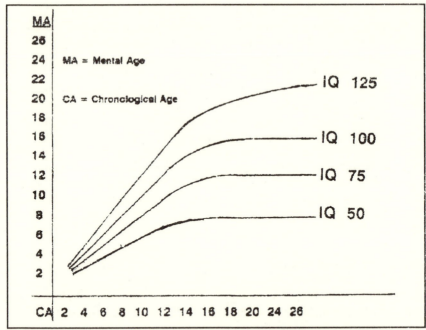

Figure 13-1. Theoretical intellectual growth patterns at different levels of IQ.

that these genes are highly variable between individuals.

The emphasis of this chapter is on variations in the time (age) of starting and leveling off of certain aspects of mental growth, not so much the rate of such growth; and although in the total population there is a high degree of correlation between early onset and rapid growth, this is not necessarily true in individual cases. In effect, a child who is precocious in mental development is likely to develop more rapidly and up to a greater age, but this is subject to variation. Due to X-linkage, such variations are likely to be greater in the case of males than of females. (The reason for this is discussed in chapter 15.)

Figure 13-2 shows (Pattern A line) what seems to be a very common variation of the usual growth pattern. The individual starts out slowly and during school years is consistently behind the average child. However, his pattern of growth for cognitive abilities, while slow during early years, continues beyond the usual age for a person of the earlier intellectual level. As a young adult, that person is within the normal range of intellectual abilities, even though he or she may have been considered mentally subnormal during school years.

Another pattern (Pattern B line) shows another type of late bloomer, but one that is less frequently seen. The child, from infancy on, is well behind

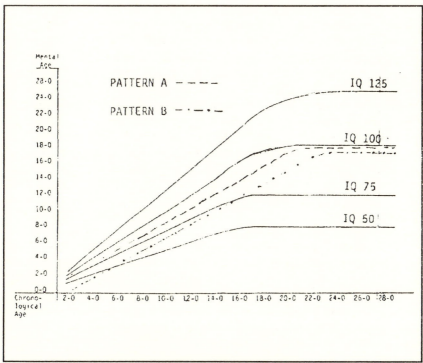

Figure 13-2. Some variations from modal growth patterns

average in cognitive ability. However, both the rate and duration of growth are similar to that of an average or superior individual. Again, the eventual growth is up to within the normal range. Later in this chapter some actual case histories of such growth patterns will be given.

The Educational Marching Society

The American educational system has been called "a great marching society". Certainly there is a strong expectation that each child should be in step with others his or her age when it comes to readiness for instruction in the three Rs. In spite of the expenditures for "special" education, in many cases inadequate provision, or inappropriate provision, seems to be made for those whose pattern of mental growth is merely out of step, especially if it is slow.

In all too many cases, children are given just one shot at learning basic educational skills. If they are not ready between the ages of 6 and 8, they are placed in special classes for the slow learner, and unless somewhere along the line they have a truly exceptional teacher, they may never be given another chance to learn the tools (reading, writing, arithmetic, and spelling) of more advanced learning. Admittedly, some schools and some parts of the country do better than others in this regard.

Even when the slow-starting child is permitted to remain in regular classes, he or she is not likely to be given the chance to make a fresh start when ready for it. The practice, in most places, is to give the slow learner "social" promotions, plus extra drill in academic subjects at the level considered appropriate to a child of his or her chronological age, and to consider the child uneducable if that doesn't result in fairly normal progress. While there is a little evidence that slow learning children do a bit better in the long run if left in regular classes, this may be because those children left in such classes are more capable than those transferred to special classes. Even in such cases, when a slow-learning child is kept in regular classes, the emotional cost of constant failure and equally constant unfavorable comparison (self-made, as often as not) in the regular class may be as serious as the labeling associated with special class placement.

To make the situation more frustrating, the individual child whose growth pattern is slow in getting started may be one of those who continue intellectual growth to a greater age, thus eventually compensating for the slow start. As an adult, he (since this is most often a male pattern) or occasionally she could be capable of handling more advanced knowledge and patterns of logic, but would be handicapped by lack of basic educational skills. The prevalence of this pattern is evidenced by some remarkable data from the British Columbia survey of handicapped children (further discussed later in this chapter), and also by other surveys from around the world.

When Mental Retardation Is Not Mental Deficiency

I prefer to reserve the term "mental retardation" for this pattern of delayed mental maturation rather than for the conditions currently being given that name. I am forced, therefore, into using what my colleagues of the American Association on Mental Retardation consider old-fashioned and pejorative terms such as "mental subnormality" or "mental deficiency" for situations in which the inadequate mental functioning continues through adult years. For purposes of this book, I choose to be precise rather than polite.

The phenomenon of the person who was considered mentally subnormal while in school but who ended up at a normal level of functioning as an adult was an extremely common one among the clients I saw for psychological testing, especially the young adults referred by the Division of Vocational Rehabilitation. In a rather small practice, I would see several such clients each year. In fact, it reached a point where, at least for a time, I was convinced that the psychologists who had been serving the local schools had been incompetent in their work, since so many of the persons that they had found dull or subnormal in intelligence turned out, as adults, to be within the normal range of intelligence. Like most psychologists, I knew of the evidence for the high degree of consistency of IQs.

However, as I thought the matter over, especially in light of the X-linkage theory, I decided that the cases I was encountering were examples of a fairly frequent pattern of mental growth. In effect, the school psychologists had probably been correct in their assessments as of the time they were made.

The problem is that the statistical evidence for constancy of IQ is based on the entire range of test scores, thus reflecting mainly the larger group in the normal and bright ranges. A child who is average in intelligence is likely to be average as an adult. The bright child is likely to be a bright adult.

But the child who is slow is not necessarily comparably slow as an adult. Suppose that at the age of 6 years a child has mental development comparable to that of an average 4-year-old. Under the original method of computing IQs, that is, mental age divided by chronological age times 100, his IQ would be 67, which is in the subnormal range. (While that old method of computing IQ has been abandoned in favor of a more precise statistical method, it still makes the concept understandable).

However, if that child continued to be 2 years behind the average child of similar age, by the time he was 14 (with a mental age of 12) his IQ would be 86, or low average. And if his mental age should continue to increase a couple of years longer than that of the average person, he would have average intelligence as an adult. In fact, even if that late growth didn't occur, the 2-year deficit in mental age would be far less significant in an adult than in a child. Using the old Binet method of computing IQ (MA/CA X 100), a 2-year deficit would result in an IQ of 67 (mildly retarded) for a child of 6, but an IQ of 87 (low average) in adult years.

When Intellectual Growth Is Out of Step

When it comes to physical growth and maturation, we tend to take substantial amounts of variation as a matter of course. But when *intellectual* growth is out of step, it is a different matter. A child who is a year or two more advanced than his or her peers is a source of pride to parents, and one who is behind is a source of distress and anxiety. Why should this be? For one thing, there is the emphasis placed on mental capabilities in our culture. Anther reason is the difficulties created by even a moderate deficit in IQ because of the rigid standards set by the school system. A child is expected to be ready to learn to read at age 6, to do simple multiplication and division by age 8, and so forth. The child who is a couple of years behind in intellectual and sensory maturation—who cannot handle the basics of reading by the age of 8, for instance—is in trouble. He or she is being taught third grade reading, without having acquired the basic skills taught in first and second grades. In effect, he or she is a non-reader, and so is at a disadvantage in acquiring the knowledge one is expected to gain by reading.

A few lucky children with this problem are put into special classes where they *may* be given a chance to start over from scratch once they have acquired the appropriate readiness levels. Most, though, are considered permanent slow learners and either given "social" promotions or put into classes where academic training is deemphasized.

Suppose, then, that a child is, in a literal sense, somewhat retarded, or behind average, in his mental growth during his (or, less often, her) early school years. That would show up as inability to handle education at the level expected of one his or her age.

Furthermore, since such students cannot handle the training they are being given in such subjects as reading and arithmetic, they lack the basics for further education. They are *educationally* deficient. That would also show up as a low score on an intelligence test, since many of the items are based on previous learning. (A person who has learned well in the past can be expected to learn well in the future.)

However, the child's pattern of intellectual development may be such that later development will enable him or her to catch up in that regard. Let me give you a couple of examples from my clinical practice that illustrate that situation.

Ricky

Ricky (not his real name) is a fairly dramatic, but not atypical, case from among those adults referred to me for evaluation during my career as a psychologist. His story is chosen because I happen to have more followup on him than on most of the others.

He was a husky, good-looking fellow, whose name and general appearance marked him as being of Mexican descent. He had attended school only until he was 16, and most of that was meaningless in an educational sense. In spite of repeating first grade, he had not learned to read or to do more than simple sums by the time he was in third grade, so from then on he was given social promotions. Had he been in a school district where there were special classes for slow learners, he might have been assigned to such a class; but ordinarily (that is, except where there were some exceptional teachers) this wouldn't have made much difference.

Ricky held a variety of low-level jobs after leaving school. He had been married and divorced, being left with the responsibility for two children. In his early 30s he was just struggling to get by.

He did have one thing going for him, though. He had a lady friend who was a bright, attractive, and energetic woman and who wasn't about to let him just drift as he had in the past. Having worked with persons who were mentally handicapped, she realized that Ricky was not in this category, and also that he was highly motivated toward self-improvement. For instance, he wanted to learn to be a welder, a skill in great demand up on the Iron Range where he lived. So, this friend came to my office one day (she worked at a hospital where I was employed part time) and asked for suggestions.

The obvious starting point was a referral to the Division of Vocational Rehabilitation, and since I was a consultant to that agency, that was easily arranged. DVR, in turn, referred him back to me for a psychological evaluation.

In view of Ricky's educational background, it was not surprising that the tests showed him to be almost totally illiterate. However, his intelligence testing was most interesting.

The most commonly used individual IQ test for adults is the Wechsler Adult Intelligence Scale (WAIS). This test has two parts, each yielding a separate IQ. Half of the test is verbal in nature, the other (performance) half is essentially non-verbal. On the verbal half of the test, Ricky's IQ was 73, down in the lower 4 percent of the population. (In technical terms he was at the fourth percentile.) This is not surprising in view of his lack of a normal educational background.

The fact that the verbal IQ reflects educational achievement should not be used as a criticism of the test, since in most cases the best predictor of future learning ability is past performance. However, as it turned out in Ricky's case, there are exceptions, and it is the job of the psychologist to determine whether the case under examination is one of these. However well verbal tests work for most people, they must be interpreted carefully in situation where the person has a language handicap or, as in Ricky's case, an educational deficit.

In such cases, a low Verbal IQ may mean only that the person couldn't read well enough to find out that there are 52 weeks in a year, in what continent Chile is located, what "conceal" means, and the like. Lack of academic *knowledge*, even when current intellectual functioning is normal, can result in a low IQ on most verbal (as contrasted with performance) tests.

On the performance half of the WAIS, Ricky's IQ was 92, at the 32nd percentile, and well within the average range. Since this half of the test involves mainly the ability to adapt to new situations and to learn from immediate experience, prior education has much less effect on the results.

In addition to the "adaptability" factor, at least two of the five performance subtests involve spatial perception and related logic. As mentioned in chapter 11, this is another X-linked intellectual factor, largely uncorrelated with verbal ability. Research with persons of overall lower-than-average IQs has shown that for such persons the Performance IQ is a better predictor of social and vocational success than is the Verbal IQ.

Under DVR sponsorship, Ricky was given a stipend that enabled him to attend the local vocational school where he received training in welding. He also made arrangements with his own school district to obtain education in reading and arithmetic, which I stressed should be started out at the first-grade level. In a few months he was reasonably competent in both.

The last I heard of him, about 2 years later, Ricky was managing his own welding business. He read his own contracts, and did his own estimating, a job requiring good arithmetic skills. His lady friend, who became his wife, was justifiably proud of his achievements.

Here, then, is an illustration of what can happen when a person (usually a male) is slower in mental maturation than his age-mates. In most cases, the problem is never dealt with appropriately, and the person carries the stigma of mental subnormality (which actually is educational deficiency) into adult years. This would be the situation diagrammed by the dashed line in figure 13-2.

Jim's Case

It should be understood that not every case of delayed intellectual develop-ment (as shown by late school readiness) that I have encountered has been due to X-linked genetic factors. In some cases disease or birth injuries have caused slow development but later on the X-linked growth pattern had a decided effect on the ultimate outcome. Jim (a pseudonym) was one such person.

An impressively good-looking young man of 25 when I saw him, he also came from a remarkable family. His father was a professor, his mother an exceptionally bright and capable college graduate, and his brothers and sis-ters all had graduate degrees. It would certainly be expected that Jim, too, would resemble his family in brilliance. However, his was a difficult birth, and he almost died in the delivery room. There was some brain damage, though not so extensive as to result in untreatable spasticity, but as Jim grew up, his developmental milestones, such as toilet training and talking, were delayed.

In school, too, he was slow. He was placed in a special class for slow learners before he finished second grade, and he remained in special classes until he finished his 12 years of education.

After graduation, where he received a certificate of attendance rather than a diploma, he was given training in janitorial and housekeeping work under a DVR (Division of Vocational Rehabilitation) program for mentally subnormal persons, but he never went into that type of work. The DVR did find him a job as a kitchen helper in a hospital, but he held that job for only a year and a half before quitting. Then for a few years he just stayed home and watched a lot of TV, especially sports, in which he was remarkably well versed. He also attended almost every sporting event of the local university.

A little later, the community advocate for the Association for Retarded Citizens followed up on the careers of special class students to determine whether their needs were being met. The advocate wasn't at all pleased to find out that Jim wasn't working, and he referred him back to DVR. That's where I came into the picture.

As I was taking down an educational and work history prior to psychological testing, Jim explained to me that he had left the hospital job "for both my physical and mental health". That didn't sound like a mentally subnormal person talking. To top it off, testing showed that Jim could read better than the average person his age. He had taught himself to read during his high school years. His arithmetic wasn't quite that good, but it was adequate for most purposes.

He took the Minnesota Multiphasic Personality Inventory (which requires at least a 6th-grade reading level) without difficulty and had a normal profile, so it can't be said that his early school failure was due to emotional problems. On the Wechsler Adult Intelligence Scale (WAIS) his Verbal, Performance and Full Scale IQs were all a little above average. Yet as a child he had been tested frequently, at both his family's and the school's insistence, and found to be intellectually subnormal, or at best marginal.

What seems to have happened is that the birth injury set his intellectual development back seriously, but that he had inherited (from his very brilliant mother, since it is an X-linked characteristic) a mental growth pattern that resulted in a more rapid pace of intellectual development and also a longer period of mental growth than is usual. In effect, his mental *growth* pattern was like that of his parents and sibs, but because of the birth injury he started at a lower point. Although he caught up, to the extent of reaching an above-average IQ for the population, he didn't end up as bright as his brothers and sisters. Sad to say, I don't know what happened subsequently, except that Jim was referred for work more appropriate to his capabilities. I suspect, though, that he is doing quite all right.

Mental Retardation

It is cases like those of Jim and Ricky that make me reserve the term "mentally retarded" for those persons whose intellectual development is delayed, or retarded, not permanently impaired. Note that in Jim's case it is likely that there would have been some degree of mental subnormality remaining in adult years had he not had a truly remarkable pattern of genetic growth of intelligence, plus a family setting that gave him encouragement and a continuing opportunity to learn and develop his capabilities.

Epidemiological Studies

Some persons are likely to say that cases like those of Jim and Ricky are rarities, and the fact that I saw so many of them was due to my interest in cognitive and learning disorders. The truth is that at the time in question I was the only source of psychological testing in much of the area I served, so all types of cases were referred to me.

In fact, there is evidence that cases of delayed mental maturation are the rule rather than the exception among children with academic problems. Numerous epidemiological studies show a pattern of increasing prevalence of mental subnormality up until the teens, and then a drop. For instance, figure 13-3, which is from an article by Dr. E. M. Gruenberg, shows that pattern in 6 out of 7 samples. The secondary peak in the 50- to 60-year age range of some studies can have many explanations. For instance, the death of parents can necessitate a diagnosis of mental deficiency in order to provide welfare assistance for some marginal persons who had previously been cared for at home.

An even better idea of the increase and decline of mental subnormality with age is shown in figure 13-4, which is based on a very thorough census of mentally subnormal persons in the Canadian province of British Columbia. Due to exceptional professional and public cooperation, the ascertainment level was almost total. That is, almost every person in the entire province, up to the age of 60, who tested in the subnormal range, or who was considered subnormal on the basis of history and current level of functioning, was counted.

The graph shows a year-by-year increase in the prevalence of mental subnormality up to the 15- to 19-year range, then a drop. The pattern is the same for both males and females, but more pronounced in the case of males, as might be expected when there is an X-linked factor involved.

The data on which figure 13-4 is based come from community sources, so it is probable that not all adults who would have tested out low (who were psychometrically subnormal only) were counted. This results in an apparent higher prevalence of mental subnormality during school years. After all, school is the toughest intellectual challenge many persons face, at least for an extended period of time, and the one most likely to use testing to rate a person's competence. Once out of school, many such persons of marginal intelligence manage to find work within their capabilities and to get along socially, and so they are no longer considered mentally handicapped.

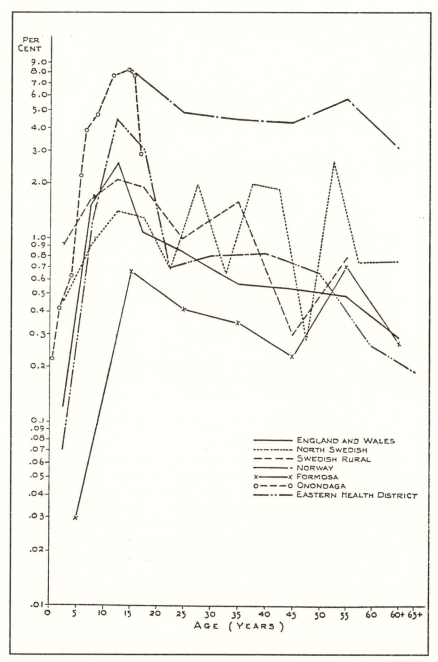

Figure 13-3. The percentage (logarithmic), by age groups, of persons considered to be mentally subnormal in some earlier epidemiological studies (1925-1956). *Source:* From "Epidemiology" by E. M. Gruenberg, Figure 1. In Stevens and Heber, Eds. (1964) *Mental Retardation*. University of Chicago Press. Reprinted by permission of the Publisher.

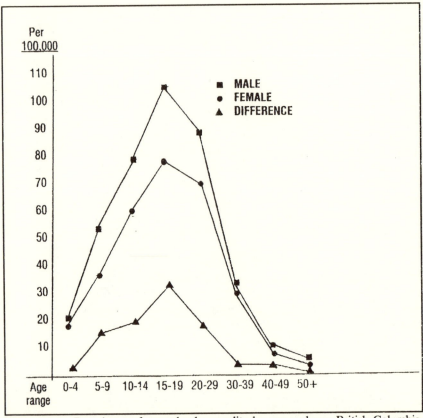

Figure 13-4. Prevalence of mental subnormality by age and sex: British Columbia, 1971.

Still, that situation by itself does not seem to be enough to explain the increase and decline in the numbers of persons considered mentally subnormal shown in figures 13-3 and 13-4. The conclusion seems inescapable that many persons, especially males, develop slowly, in an intellectual sense, up until their teens, but their intellectual growth continues for a while longer, bringing their functioning up to the normal range during adult years. In such cases, an educational rather than intellectual deficit is probably the greatest handicap.

It should be noted that the 1976 and subsequent censuses of handicapping conditions for British Columbia showed a peak for the prevalence of mental subnormality at a much later age. However, an extraneous factor had been introduced into the situation, a subsidy for adults classified as "retarded". An adult who, on a psychometric or social basis, qualified for this subsidy was automatically included in the count, even though under previous standards he or she might not have been.

Race Differences

Now, here's where I stick my neck out. I'm going to get into the subject of "racial" differences in intelligence. I do so because certain corollaries of the X-linkage theory may offer something positive in the way of dealing with what is definitely a problem. In other words, there may be something we can do to minimize the effects of group differences in the abilities related to academic achievement.

And I do mean that I am sticking my neck out. An acquaintance of mine, Dr. Arthur Jensen, who is an outstanding scholar and a fine person, for a long time had to be accompanied by a bodyguard as he traveled around the campus of an excellent university, California Berkeley. What was the problem? He had stated, almost incidentally, in a publication in a relatively obscure journal (*The Harvard Educational Review*), that black children tended to score lower on intelligence tests than did white children, and that black children did not, on an average, do as well in school as white.

Another person, Dr. Frank McGurk, was implicitly threatened with excommunication from his church if he continued to discuss the findings from his doctoral dissertation that blacks, on an average, did not do as well as whites on intelligence tests, even if social class was held constant. For instance, children of black upper-middle-class families did not do as well, overall, as children of white upper-middle-class families.

Now there is no question that such findings are true, although there is a lot of disagreement over *why* they are true. The sin of Jensen, McGurk and others is that they *publicly* discussed these well-established facts, and these facts are disturbing to many people, who learned early in life to take literally the philosophy that "all people are created equal". They don't stop to think that this is a moral concept, not a scientific fact. Yet without the facts, or with incorrect ideas, how are people of good will going to deal with the situation? A lot of people, campus liberals prominent among them, have tended to react in the manner of the king of ancient times who had the messenger bearing bad news killed.

But what good does it do to try and cover up or deny scientific findings? Without knowledge of the true situation, how are intelligent people going to seek the reasons behind it? And without *that* knowledge, how are public officials going to apply intelligent solutions to the problem? The situation is a biological fact, for which no-one or no group is to blame, and which no legislation is going to eliminate.

An analogy might help. What if some pressure group decided to enforce the idea that it is cruel and inhuman, and denying of human rights, for a doctor to tell a patient that he or she has cancer. Without that knowledge, the patient would not only fail to seek appropriate treatment, but would not be able to make suitable plans for his or her family.

Is Desegregation the Answer?

Among the things Jensen pointed out in his *Harvard Educational Review* article (1969a, 1969b) was that the huge study regarding racial factors in education done by Dr. James Coleman (1966) did not take into account certain genetic factors that would make its findings questionable and its recommendations invalid. Nonetheless, because of lack of adequate information, or possibly in disregard of the information available, the courts proceeded, on the basis of the Coleman study, to order school desegregation.

A dozen years later, Dr. Coleman himself admitted that his conclusions regarding the reasons for the blacks' lower educational achievement were faulty. In other words, on the basis of incorrectly interpreted data, the courts had, in effect, passed a law affecting all of the schools in the country. It doesn't take a statistician or a college professor to see the dangers in thus acting on an incorrect assessment of a situation. The editorial on the next page, which was copied (with permission) directly from the Duluth (MN) *Herald* for Sept. 18, 1978 presents the views of an intelligent journalist on the subject.

Nor does it do any good to admit the fact that many children are not obtaining an adequate education and then simply try to place the blame for the situation on individual people or public institutions such as schools. Blaming does not help solve problems. In fact, to the extent that genetic factors are involved in the matter of racial differences, there is no basis for blame. A person cannot be held responsible for his or her genes, or for those of other people. With a few exceptions, human genes (unlike those of domesticated plants or animals) are not under any type of personal or social control.

Social Control of the Genes for Intelligence

Perhaps they should be, at least in some cases. For instance, does a person who has a high risk of having a mentally subnormal child have an absolute right to bear children? What if that person is too mentally defective to care for a child? As an example, I have worked with a case where a child was born to a mildly subnormal woman from a family in which there were two different sex-linked disorders. Her first child, a boy, was normal, and was placed in a foster home, and she herself was placed in an institution for the retarded as a substitute for sterilization, since the State insisted that she wasn't competent to consent to sterilization (she underwent sterilization by institutionalization, if you will!).

Many years later she was placed in a community setting, where as a consequence of a back-room tryst with one of the employees at her work place,

Busing backfires

It takes courage to admit a mistake, and the bigger the mistake, the more courage.

In this light, socialolgist-educator James Coleman is a brave man.

It was Coleman who, in 1966, issued a report on education in America which added momentum to the national effort to integrate schools. Coleman's 1966 report was based in studying 600,000 students and 60,000 teachers in 4,000 schools. The conclusion, in simplest form, was that the social-class composition of a school had more impact on learning than did teachers and teaching methods.

Said another way, Coleman concluded that black and underprivileged children could benefit from being educated with middle and upperclass white children because of the educational resources these white children brought to school from their home, and because of the relatively higher degree of motivation they brought from their home.

The so-called "Coleman Report" gave great academic credibility to the nation's efforts to integrate classrooms. We were not forcing integration simply for social reasons, but for educational reasons as well. Through the Coleman report, the nation concluded that black children would become better educated in integrated classrooms.

Now, however, Coleman has reversed himself. Now a professor of sociology at the University of Chicago, Coleman has issued a new report in which he concludes, "it is not the case that school desegregation, as it has been carried out in American schools, generally brings achievement benefits to disadvantaged children." Although he argued 12 years ago that "integration would bring about achievement benefits," he said, "it has not worked out this way...Thus, what once appeared to be fact is now known to be fiction.

"Desegregation has turned out to be much more complicated than any of us ever realized," Coleman said. What caused the reversal of his theory? The cause, according to Coleman, is his disccovery that there are different results from forced, as opposed to voluntary, desegregation. In integrated schools which brought black and white children together simply because the children lived in common neighborhoods, he said, black children generally benefitted from the mixed classroom setting. Mandatory integration, however, which brought black and white children together from widely separated neighborhoods, Coleman said, has not benefited black students. "There appear to be beneficial effects for some black kids," he said, "those who are better students, and harmful effects for blacks who are poorer students."

Coleman's general position now is to be opposed to legally segregated schools, but at the same time not in favor of integrated schools which are the result of forced busing. Thus, we continue to deal with a problem which has no easy answers. It is constructive, nevertheless, to discover that one of the attempted solutions—mandatory busing across great distances— is, in Coleman's words, "counterproductive."

Editorial from the Duluth (Minn.) Herald for Sept. 18, 1978. (Copied with permission.)

she bore a second son. My examination of that son when he was just a week or two old showed that he had the same type of hydrocephalus as two of his uncles. He was placed for foster care with an older couple who were aware that he would be mentally deficient. However, a few years later it became apparent that he had also inherited the gene for the Duchenne type of muscular dystrophy, which slowly progresses to total paralysis and invariably an early death. The emotional trauma to the loving foster parents must have been extreme, and that doesn't take into account the financial cost of his support, which was borne by the taxpayers.

In that case the state involved was so concerned about the "rights" of a mentally subnormal woman that surgical sterilization was denied her since she was assumed not to have enough intelligence to consent legally. (Instead, they literally locked her up for 20 years.) The State's decision denied her the right *not* to have children she couldn't care for. It also denied the people of the state a chance to protect themselves from the totally unproductive costs of rearing a profoundly handicapped child. They also tried (with limited success) to deny her the right to a normal sex life.

The Longer View

Now to get back to the topic of dealing with large numbers of children whose developmental schedule is substantially slower than average. Numerically (in this country), the majority of such children are Caucasian, but proportionally there are greater numbers of racial minorities (other than Oriental and Middle-Eastern). While modifying the educational system so that its schedules of teaching are adapted to the individual students may be helpful in the short run, the problem (if it is a problem) of differences in average test and academic scores between ethnic groups will probably have to wait for a solution until enough generations have passed for a complete blending of racial groups in our society. This may not be as far off as it may appear, but it is still much too remote to be considered a solution for present-day problems. In fact, in view of the trend for the less intelligent persons in the community to have larger numbers of offspring, this will probably result in an overall lowering of the intellectual level in the United States. That is a matter that has been discussed in such books as *The Bell Curve* (Herrnstein and Murray, 1994) and need not be gone into here.

In the past, the existence of large numbers of persons of subaverage intelligence has not been a serious problem. It has been my experience that high verbal intelligence is as much a liability as an asset to a person who must earn a living at many industrial and agricultural jobs today. Nonetheless, the criteria for "success" are set by persons with higher education or those who have managed to succeed economically and vocationally. The superintendent of schools feels that students should receive the same type of education that got him to his lofty place in the world, if at all possible. And, to be honest, more and more of present-day jobs do require at least a moderate level of cognitive ability and education. It has not always been thus. The best paid of the students of my own high school class, back in 1935, was by far the dumbest in the English classes. He worked, even while he was still in school, as a boilermaker on the locomotives at the railroad roundhouse.

However, things have changed, and computers and power equipment have replaced clerical ability and brawn. To make matters worse, the idea of pride in one's ability to do hard physical labor has almost disappeared. Nowadays, at least in the parts of the country in which I have spent my life, the tedious and physically demanding jobs are frequently filled by Mexicans. Intellectual and educational deficits are more and more of a handicap.

A Possible Solution

Here's where the idea of the X-linked growth factor comes in. If it actually is the case that a substantial part of the differences in IQ and school achievement are due to a different *timetable* of mental development, rather than to some fixed level of mental capability, our well-meant attempts to integrate schools could have exactly the wrong effect. Such integration seems to have resulted in timetables for teaching that are inappropriate for increasingly large numbers of children. In schools serving a relatively homogeneous population, the teachers have at least some chance of suiting the curriculum to the needs of the majority of the students—that is, provided the school administration gives them the leeway.

For instance, it has been noted (and duly reported by Jensen, Coleman, and others) that by the fourth year of school, black children are, on an average, about one academic year behind white children in basic educational level. But, does this mean that the black children are permanently less capable of learning, or does it mean that their mental development is on a schedule that is later than, but not necessarily inferior to, that of the white children? Quite possibly it is a combination of the two.

In any case, would it not be more humane, and more effective, to group the children, regardless of racial background, according to their needs, permitting all of the students to learn at the pace that stimulates their learning without discouraging it? The segregation (nasty word nowadays) would be based on the child's rate and level of development, not on the color of his or her skin.

Frankly, I doubt that this is the total answer, but there is some evidence that it does give at least a partial solution. In the September 1978 issue of the *Readers' Digest,* an article by Sidney H. Stapleton told of a school in the South where a child (black or white) was not passed on to the next grade until he showed reasonable competence in the basic academic subjects at each grade level. Over the years this seems to have had good results. While many schools throughout the nation are denying graduation to those students who fail to pass basic tests of literacy, graduation seems far too late to make this determination. Wouldn't it be a lot more humane, and much more effective, to administer the necessary tests early, and as often as necessary, to assure that a child is ready before being passed on to the next grade.

Because, in the school reported in the *Digest,* such testing resulted in more black than white students being held back, there had been criticism of it. However, the article included a very telling quotation from the school board's only black member, a successful business man.

> I had been hiring local high school graduates for years, and I knew many of them couldn't read or spell properly. I was troubled by the kind of schooling my own kids were getting. Under Sam's [the school superintendent] plan, more black students might be held back. But I felt holding them back could be the best way for them to catch up—better than allowing them to get out into the world uneducated, where they'd never have a chance to catch up.

"They'd never have a chance to catch up." That seems to be the problem faced by millions of children of all races whose schedule of mental development is slower than that of the average child. This does not always mean that they lack the capacity for catching up. Some of them, like Ricky in the case history above, could have a pattern of mental growth that is slow in starting but which continues for more than the usual number of years, giving them as adults a normal level of intellect and learning ability. But unless they get a chance to learn basic educational skills *after* their readiness is established, they are likely to remain educationally handicapped throughout their lives.

It may be, too, that simply holding back a child for a year or two or three, or even more, is not enough. Many children do learn to read and do arithmetic later on, but they still carry such negative feelings about these skills that throughout their lives they hate to read or do calculations, all because of the feelings of frustration and failure as well-meaning teachers tried to force them into something that was, at the time, a *physical* (not just a mental) impossibility for them. In other words, it may be better to give a child who is slow in developing a holiday from academic work until testing or observation shows that he or she is ready for it.

Or perhaps we could take a lesson from Denmark. There most children don't start academic classes until they are 8 years old, and then they attend classes only half days for the first 2 years. Even so, by the time they reach their teens they are on the same academic level as children of the same age in the United States. The limiting factor in school achievement, especially at the early grade levels, is intellectual and physiological maturation, not years of schooling. It is one of the great cruelties of our times that we are insisting that children of all races, but an especially large proportion of blacks, fit into a schedule of education that is based on the average rate of development of middle- and upper-class whites.

It occurs to me that we would have a real riot on our hands if we insisted that all school children follow a curriculum based on the capabilities of the Oriental students. Their rate of maturation during school years, it seems, is about as far ahead of the Caucasian students' as the Caucasian students' is ahead of the blacks'. The same can probably be said about Jewish students. There may also be differences in specific areas of superiority (Seligman, 1992) including certain "right-brain" functions.

People who are acquainted with the literature on racial differences in cognitive and test abilities are likely to point out that it is not just blacks but also Chicanos and American Indians, that are likely to be below the average white in IQ. The average deficits for these two groups seem to be about half of those of the blacks.

However, it may be that the deficits reported in minority groups, as adults, are due in large part to inappropriate scheduling of classroom instruction, on the basis of chronological age rather than readiness. In our competitive society we are pressured to move ahead full speed in educational programs, without regard to the needs of individual students.

The "Rose" County Study

For instance, the huge "Rose" County (a fictitious name) study (Imre, 1968) by Drs. Lemkau and Imre showed that even as adults, blacks are more than a dozen times more likely to be classified as mentally subnormal (IQ below 70) as are whites.

In that study, the entire adult population up to age 60 (7,475 persons) of a Maryland county was screened for mental deficiency. As might be expected, males were more likely than females to be classified mentally subnormal. The male:female ratio for whites was 1.69 : 1.02; and for blacks, 21.57 : 16.49 (per 100 adults in the population).

In this county, 56 percent of the population was white. Of these, as previously mentioned, 1.69 percent of the males and 1.02 percent of the females were classified as subnormal in intelligence. But the percentage of mental subnormals among the black males was 21.57, almost 13 times the proportion for white males. The percentage for black females was 16.49, over 16 times the proportion for white females. Over all, in this county, an adult black was about 14 times as likely to be considered mentally defective as an adult white.

Probably this very thorough study *does* mean that blacks have a lower average intelligence level than whites. However, the difference in actual intelligence, as opposed to intelligence test scores, could be much smaller, if one takes into account the manner in which the study was done.

The test used was the verbal portion of the Wechsler Adult Intelligence Scale (WAIS). This is individually administered, and it requires no ability at reading or writing. But, as previously pointed out, it is highly dependent on educational background, with questions based on American history, geography, arithmetic, vocabulary, and the like.

A person who had not been ready to learn to read while in the early grades of school, the only time it was offered, would not have had the basic skills needed for further learning, and so would not have the educational background considered normal for a person educated in the U.S. school system. Consequently he or she would not do well on such a test. As a child, he or she would have been shunted off to special education, or simply passed from grade to grade, anything to get him (or her) out of the school setting as expeditiously as possible. As an adult, that person would be virtually certain to have an *educational* deficit that could show up as a low verbal IQ, and which would also limit his or her social and economic functioning in some respects.

Alternative Educational Schedules

In essence, a large part of the problem of blacks' and other minorities' lower achievement levels (outside of sports, that is) may be the educational deficits resulting from inappropriate school curricula. It really does no good, except possibly in a social and nutritional sense (providing well-balanced lunches), to start children in a school setting before they are ready for it. Perhaps we could take another lesson from Denmark in this matter. There, because of high living costs, and especially, high taxes, most mothers are forced to work. Because children do not ordinarily start in school until the age of 8, and then only for half days for the first two years, some system of child care is needed. At least in the larger cities, there are day care centers, *creches* for infants and *kindergartens* for children from ages 3 to 8, where many children are taken during daytime hours. Here the children spend their time as suits their own preferences, in active play, in simple games, and in taking care of their own needs. For instance, in a kindergarten I visited there was a child-size sink where children washed their own dishes after lunch. Some of the older children played simple games with cards having large, easily readable numbers on them, but there were no educational programs, per se. Still, Danish children are on an educational par with those in the United States by the time they are in their early teens, or even before. It is the child's level of maturation, not the number of years in school, that determine readiness for each grade level.

The Danes may have discovered what we have not. Formal education does no good, in fact, there is clinical evidence that it is harmful, if it is forced on children before they are ready for it. We are aware that teaching a youngster to throw a curve ball before he or she is physically ready to do so can cause damage that can keep him or her from ever becoming a capable pitcher. Why must we force children into trying to learn academic skills before they are physiologically ready and thereby possibly turn them off from educational pursuits for the rest of their lives?

The Actual Effects of Integration

By creating a situation that does exactly that, the courts' integration programs have created a situation that does just the opposite of what was intended. Under the pressure of poorly informed public opinion, zealot school administrators continue to set quotas and pressure teachers into advancing students, ready or not, and even to condone or encourage cheating on the aptitude tests given in order to cover up the lack of positive results.

While I was spending a few very happy weeks as a visiting professor at the College of William and Mary in Williamsburg, Virginia, the school systems in that vicinity were being racially integrated as a result of the Supreme Court decision. Many of my students were teachers or teachers' aides in those schools. While most of them had strong feelings, one way or the other, about the situation, out of respect for their employers they did not talk much about it.

However, the matter of teaching strategy was brought up frequently. In the Norfolk schools, the largest of the systems, there had been a pronounced discrepancy in academic achievement levels between the "black" and "white" schools. At the fourth grade level, for instance, the students from the predominantly white districts were at about the national norms for that grade, while those from the black districts were about a year below grade level. How was a teacher to deal with that situation in the integrated schools? If he or she taught at the regular fourth grade level, the slower students would be left to flounder with work for which they were unprepared, leaving them even farther behind at the end of the year. Or, if the teacher worked with the slower students, the advanced students would be left to twiddle their thumbs and get into mischief. If the teacher divided up class time between the groups, no-one would get full benefit, and the exceptional students at both the high and low ends would be relatively neglected.

Within a school system, the problem might be solved by use of a track system, by which students are grouped according to ability. However, with this goes a lot of the integration sought by such groups as the N.A.A.C.P. (National Association for Advancement of Colored Persons). Furthermore there arises a problem of teacher assignment. It has been my own experience that schools that have experimented with such systems have not kept them long because of serious problems with staffing. Practically every teacher wants to be assigned the upper tracks where the work is more stimulating.

It should not be inferred, however, that differences in the rate of intellectual maturation occur on a strictly racial basis. They are universal. The very traits that show up with racial differences are the ones that also show the greatest variation *within* a race or group. The blacks don't have a monopoly on "dumbth" by any means.

And when physical coordination and strength are taken into account, the total functioning level of the blacks goes way up. Just watch any football, basketball or baseball game at the college or professional level.

Chapter 14

Inheritance of X-linked Traits

Hypothesis 11. Because a boy receives his only X-chromosome from his mother, the adage, "Like father, like son," does not apply to cognitive and to other X-linked abilities to the same extent as to traits related to autosomal genes.

Like Father, Like Son?

It may come as a shock to some but, based on a theory of X-linkage of major intellectual traits, for many highly valued intellectual traits the saying, "Like father, like son," does not hold true. A male child receives his only X-chromosome from his mother. From his father, the boy receives only a tiny Y-chromosome which, so far as is known, carries few or no genes besides those for maleness and to remedy the absence of a second X-chromosome. That suggests that a father has little to do, in a genetic sense, with his sons' cognitive, spatial perception, high-level mathematical and musical abilities, and perhaps others.

In a practical sense, however, there is a significant correlation between fathers' and sons' IQs, although not as large as between mothers' and sons' (Lehrke, 1972a, 1978). This is not due to the father's genetic contribution but to the fact that, in our society at least, there is a high degree of assortative mating for intelligence. Overall, husbands and wives, who have few variable genes in common, tend to be more similar in IQ than are their children who have up to half of their variable genes in common (Lehrke, 1978).

In fact, there are what anthropologists call "breeding pools" that make this happen. There are breeding pools that lead to the meeting and mating of people with mostly lower intelligence. We call them "slums" or "low socio-economic neighborhoods". There are others where bright people meet and mate. We call them "colleges" or "universities". Of course, not all match-making occurs in such contexts, but overall there is a marked tendency for like to mate with like in an intellectual sense (Lehrke, 1978).

As long ago as 1932, a British scientist with the fascinating name of Sir Lancelot Hogben pointed out the importance of this concept. "If an appreciable proportion of the total variation [in intelligence] is due to sex-linked genes, it is of more importance that a boy should have a clever mother than a clever father." (quoted in McKusick, 1964, p. 22). In effect, a man is wise who selects (to the extent that he does the selecting) an intelligent mother for his children, especially the boys.

Family Similarities and X-Linkage

One line of evidence that would suggest X-linkage of major intellectual traits is whether intrafamily correlations of appropriate tests, such as tests of cognitive functioning, are of the degree one might expect of an X-linked trait. Bayley (1966, p. 102), in evaluating a somewhat different hypothesis, has provided the necessary data for such a test.

From a collection of intelligence test scores for family groups compiled by Outhit (1933), Bayley (1966) selected families in which there were IQ scores for both parents, as well as for a son and a daughter. What would be expected, if there are major genes relating to intelligence on the X-chromosome, is that the correlations of test scores for mother-daughter, mother-son and father-daughter would be somewhat similar. In each case, the parent and child have one X-chromosome in common. The correlations between fathers and sons should be lower, since they have no X-chromosome in common; and the brother-sister correlation should be intermediate since they have a chromosome in common half the time.

To quote Bayley (1966, p. 102):

> The resulting correlations . . . are, again, higher for the daughters than the sons. The mother-daughter r is .68, the father-daughter r is .66; The mother-son r is .61, and the father-son r is .44. The fact that the parents in this sample are the same for both sons and daughters makes this a potentially crucial test. Tests of significance (the brother-sister r is .55) indicate that these differences in father-child correlations approach significance at the .05 level.

In other words, the order of size of the correlations is exactly what might be expected of X-linked traits. If one takes into account that the rank order of the first three correlations (for mother-daughter, father-daughter, and mother-son) is not critical, there are 6 out of 120 possible permutations that fit the hypothesis. This makes the Bayley data significant at the .05 level as a test of the X-linkage of intelligence.

Additional information from the original source increases the importance of the differences. According to Outhit (1933, p. 43) the correlation between mothers and fathers in this study was .741 ± .042. In other words, the entire correlation between father and son, who have no X-chromosome in common, can be accounted for by the product of the correlation between the parents and that between mother and son (.74 times .61 = .45, as compared with a direct father-son correlation, as reported by Outhit, of 0.44).

Problems in Studying Intrafamily Correlations

It certainly would be preferable to cite numerous family studies testing the hypothesis of X-linkage of major intellectual traits by intra-family correlations. However, the best study (Outhit, 1933, cited above) was not specifically designed with that in mind.

Kamin (Eysenck and Kamin, 1981) does mention several other studies of intrafamily correlations that have been done, not all of which gave the same rank order of intra-family correlations as the Outhit data. However, due to the difficulties involved in compiling such data, this isn't surprising. For instance, intelligence test batteries don't measure quite the same abilities for children and adults, even though they may have the same name (for example, Wechsler, Stanford-Binet). In the Outhit study, this was minimized by selecting the oldest son and daughter as much as possible, but even so the test items were not entirely comparable. Finding and testing substantial numbers of families consisting of two parents and two opposite-sex children is another problem. Statistically, the range of outcomes is limited by the tendency for husbands' and wives' IQs to correlate highly, thus making it difficult to obtain significant results. In other words, meaningful parent-child correlation studies are hard to come by.

Dr. Gillian Turner (1996) points out that high intelligence, as well as low, does segregate in the pattern of sex linkage, at least in some families. She uses the example of the family of Charles Darwin and his cousin Francis Galton, in whose lineage there were at least three generations of male geniuses traced in the female line. She adds that when a man selects a bride, "His frontal cortex should interpose reminding him that his sons' intelligence, if that is important to him, is solely dependent on his partner" (p. 1815).

Chapter 15

Sex Differences in Variance

Hypothesis 12. Even more significant, X-linkage can be expected to lead to greater male variability in those areas of intellect that are X-linked. The greater number of males at the highest levels of accomplishment, then, is not entirely a matter of chauvinism and sexual politics. Neither is the greater prevalence of mental subnormality and learning disorders among males primarily a social and behavioral phenomenon.

In 1748, Lord Chesterfield, the English author and statesman, described women as "only children of larger growth". Fortunately for him, England was not ruled by a queen at the time; and women's lib had not yet come into the picture. It is only during the last century that the idea of the intellectual superiority of males has been widely questioned, much less subjected to scientific scrutiny.

The Superiority of Females

At present, though, there are many psychologists, not all of them women, who agree with Dr. David Wechsler, a leader in the intelligence testing field, who once said that "we have more than a 'sneaking suspicion' that the female of the species is not only more deadly, but also more intelligent than the male." Nonetheless, Dr. Wechsler, like Dr. Lewis Terman, another designer of intelligence tests, systematically eliminated from his tests those items that seemed to favor one sex over the other.

In fact, in spite of efforts of test designers to equalize *average* test scores between the sexes, mean differences in IQ between them continue to show up in surveys. For instance, as part of one of the largest surveys of intelligence, Drs. Elizabeth and Sheldon Reed (1965) compared the IQs of 1866 married couples and concluded that femininity is not only conducive to longer life, but also to higher intelligence as it is measured by IQ tests.

In 1971, Dr. Arthur Jensen came up with much the same result. On the basis of studies involving the administration of almost 20,000 tests of different types, it was noted that females scored, on an average, the equivalent of one IQ point higher than males. Small as that difference may seem, it would indicate that there are more than 1 percent more females than males with IQs above 100.

There can be, and probably are, many reasons for this. For one thing, little girls, up to the early teens, develop faster than boys. Since the brain and nervous system are part of the body, this more rapid growth pattern would give them an advantage on certain types of test items, just as they undoubtedly have in school work. If the Reed and Reed (1965) data, which showed that wives tend to be higher in IQ than their husbands, are applicable to the general population, it would seem that this advantage carries over to later years as well.

The difference in the rate of maturation between boys and girls could have an additional effect as a result of the American school system. A child, most likely a boy, who is physiologically not ready for basic education skills is pushed along in school at almost the same rate as those who *are* ready. He is promoted from first grade, regardless of whether he has acquired basic skills (unless the case is very obvious) and finds himself in second grade, not only physically and mentally behind most of his classmates in terms of maturation, but lacking in essential basic skills needed to get along in that grade. That process may be a major part of the reason that boys are 2 to 3 times as likely to fail in school as are girls.

However, in the middle teens the boys catch up with the girls in physical development and so, if it is only a matter of physical and physiological maturation, the numbers of persons with school problems should start to even out between the sexes. But they don't. One very large study by A. B. Baker, which was cited in my earlier publication, *Sex Linkage: A Biological Basis for Greater Male Variability in Intelligence* (Lehrke, 1978), showed that nationwide there were still almost 75 percent more boys than girls in special education classes at the high school level.

As suggested earlier in this book (chapter 13), this may be a carryover from early special class placement. That is, a child, once placed in a special class, receives a different level of training that does not qualify him or her for return to regular classes even though there may have been a relative increase in intellectual functioning.

Dr. Nancy Bayley (1966) came up with another possible explanation of the greater numbers of mentally subnormal and learning disordered males.

She pointed out that males are not only more subject to disease but are more likely to experience severe effects from their illnesses. She suggested also that they may be more sensitive to conditions such as birth injury, malnutrition, poor home environment, and the like, that could lead to decreased intelligence. Because of their basic genetic inferiority in such respects (which could be sex-linked), it would be expected that more boys than girls would suffer from physical problems involving the brain or central nervous system that would result in their being dull or subnormal.

The High End of the Scale

However, Dr. Bayley's theory explains only those types of deficit that have an organic basis. It does not seem to be related to that group of mentally deficient persons for whom there is no identifiable organic basis, those of the so-called cultural-familial type. Furthermore, it doesn't explain why there are more males than females with markedly *high* levels of intelligence.

There has probably been some strong evidence of this greater male variability in the archives of test designers, although up until recently there seems to have been an effort to keep such data secret because making it public would make it appear that their test is unfair to women. For instance, while the designers of the original Wechsler Adult Intelligence Scale went to great lengths to demonstrate that their tests did not discriminate against either males or females as far as *average* scores is concerned, they said nothing about sex differences in *variability*. The only clue one gets that such a difference exists is that on 10 of the 11 subtests of the WAIS the standard deviation for males is higher. The single exception is the Coding subtest, part of the Performance portion of the test. Until recently, the practice of ignoring sex differences in variance seems to have continued in the documentation of virtually all major intelligence tests.

Nonetheless, empirical evidence of the excess of males at the high end of the scale abounds. The most famous study involving the high range of IQs was done in the middle 1920s by Dr. Louis Terman (1925), who made a thorough search for all of the brightest children in the California schools. He found 37 percent more boys than girls with IQs at the markedly superior level, above 140. In fact, he said, "the facts we have presented are in harmony with the hypothesis that exceptionally superior intelligence occurs with greater frequency among boys than among girls".

This impression was based on actual evidence. In his huge study of exceptionally bright school children, Terman found a male : female ratio of 1.2 to 1 for those being evaluated for his study of children at the genius level.

Dr. Anne Anastasi, in her textbook on individual psychological differences (*Differential Psychology*, 3d edition, 1958, p. 628), suggested that the excess of boys in Terman's study might have been due to selection bias on the part of the teachers.

> It should be noted that the children in the California study were located in large part through teachers' recommendations. . . . It is thus likely that the excess of boys in the California group resulted from the effects of sex stereotypes on teachers' judgment. Perhaps a girl with a high IQ was more often regarded by her teachers as a "good pupil," while a boy with the same IQ was judged to be "brilliant".

However, Dr. Anastasi missed out on a comparison that suggests that the bias was actually in the opposite direction. The original group, selected, as she says, through teachers' recommendations, consisted of 857 boys and 671 girls. However, after actual psychological testing of each of these students, there remained 813 boys with IQs above 140, or 95 percent of the original group; but only 592 girls, or 88 percent of the original group. That is, there were actually 37 percent more brilliant boys than girls when it came to objective scores.

Now, however, there is more recent evidence of greater male variability at the high end of the scale. Gilder (1995) reported that on the Graduate Record Examination, an intelligence test designed for use with applicants for graduate school placement, a score in the quantitative aptitude section that placed women at the 92d percentile among women would place males only at the 62d percentile among men. While this particular section of the test reflects primarily mathematical functioning, an area where males have traditionally excelled, other sections tend in the same direction. For instance, table 15.1, which is based on the scores of 381,200 persons who took the Graduate Record Examination in 1992 and 1993, shows that the average scores for males exceeded that for females in all three areas of the test. Furthermore, males had a greater standard deviation on all three areas, an even stronger indication of greater male variability.

Thus, what evidence there is suggests that there are more males in the highest ranges of IQ. Certainly, as was shown in some of my earlier works on X-linkage (summarized in tables 12.1 and 12.2), there is no question but that there are more males at the low range. In other words, *males are more variable than females*.

The idea of greater male variability in intelligence is certainly not a new one. In the third edition of his book entitled *Man and Woman*, published in 1904 (p. 425), Havelock Ellis said: "We have, therefore, to recognize that in man, as in males generally, there is an organic variational tendency to diverge from the average, in women, as in females generally, an organic tendency, notwithstanding all their facility for minor oscillations, to stability and conservatism, involving diminished individualism and variability."

Table 15.1. Graduate Record Examination scores by sex, 1992-1993. *Source*: Educational Testing Service (1994). Table A.1 in *Sex, Race, Ethnicity, and Performance on the GRE® General Test.*

		Verbal	Quantitative	Analytical
Group	Number	Mean score	Mean score	Mean score
Men	169,068	486 (SD=121)	603 (SD=135)	547 (SD=133)
Women	212,132	475 (SD=111)	510 (SD=128)	532 (SD=125)
Total	381,200*	478 (SD=117)	557 (SD=140)	539 (SD=129)

* Of 416,061 examinees who took the test, 381,288 (92%) responded to the questions in this table.

This greater male variability included, in his estimation, mental processes: "It is undoubtedly true that the greater variational tendency in the male is a psychic as well as a physical fact."

A few scientists of more recent date have also accepted the idea of male variability in intelligence. Dr. Lionel Penrose (1963, p. 186), well known for his studies in the genetics of intelligence, has said, "The larger range of variation in males than in females for general intelligence is an outstanding phenomenon."

The greater male variability has also been noted in several large-scale testing programs. In 1945, Roberts, Norman and Griffiths reported on some studies of entire populations of school children in Scotland. It was their opinion that boys had at least a 13 percent greater variance than girls, and that 17 percent, or even more, would be a better estimate. Since one of the studies involved over 87,000 children, this finding is hard to question.

Dr. Arthur Jensen who, as mentioned earlier, summarized several large-scale studies of test scores in the United States (Jensen, 1971) found that although girls were a little brighter on an average, the boys had about 13 percent greater variability in the white population and 23 percent more in the black population. The 13 percent figure for U.S. whites is highly comparable to that of Roberts' Scottish population (Roberts, Norman, and Griffiths, 1945), so it is probably not just a regional phenomenon. And, like the Scottish data, even the figures Jensen reports are probably conservative. When his data from table 18 of his 1971 article are refigured, omitting data for tests that are not primarily intellectual in nature, the standard deviation of the test scores turns out to be 15 percent greater for white males than for white females; and 29 percent greater for black males than for black females.

However, in recent years the idea of greater male variability in intelligence has not received much attention. One reason might be that the leading college textbooks on individual differences, including those of Dr. Anne Anastasi and Dr. Leona Tyler, have tended to play down the likelihood of an actual difference. Even more important, there has been, up to now, no clear logical (or biological) reason to believe that such a difference *should* exist. Without such a reason, most psychologists were inclined to believe that the noted excess in numbers of males at both the high and low ends of the scale was due to social factors rather than intrinsic ones.

The question that now comes up is how a theory of X-linkage of growth-controlling genes for intelligence provides such biological evidence that males *should* be more variable.

We'll have to start with the assumption of a primitive, physiological substrate for intelligence. The genes for this basic intelligence could be, and probably are, scattered over most of the human's 46 chromosomes. The substrate (the cognitive makeup of *Homo erectus*) would permit a level of ability to learn from experience and teaching (essentially operant learning) that may be only slightly below that of modern Man. There probably was a limited amount of foresight, some capability for solving simple problems, and communication skills at a concrete level. Even at this primitive level there must have been some variation, not only between individuals but between populations, although a million or so years of evolutionary selection must have cleared out the less satisfactory alleles from the genotype.

As a result of a neotenous mutation (Adam, again), the growth of these abilities (or specifically of the neuronal interconnections related to them) was greatly extended, resulting in greater complexity. However, that gene, being basically unstable, as mentioned in chapter 7, soon became highly variable in its expression. In effect, some alleles of the genes on the X-chromosome were more effective than others in promoting the over-all growth of neuronal interconnections, and consequently on the growth of intelligence. There were undoubtedly differences in the patterns of growth as well, some areas being affected more strongly than others, thus creating differences between individuals in special abilities.

Add to that the fact that half of the descendants of a particularly intelligent male, the sons and their descendants, would not receive the superior X-chromosome. Higher intelligence, in times past, may have increased the number of children a male might have and bring to maturity (see chapter 9), but only about half of these (the daughters) would carry the superior X-linked genes in the first generation, and only a fourth of the offspring in the second generation.

Furthermore, from an evolutionary standpoint, these changes must have occurred with such recency that a high degree of selection has not yet been reached. There are several reasons for this, other than the shortness of the evolutionary period. For one thing, even the less favorable variations resulted in levels of ability that were more than adequate for survival and reproduction, at least in those environments most favorable for humans. Nor did the more favorable levels of cognition confer such high levels of adaptation that in a few thousand generations they have become extremely prevalent.

For a model that will illustrate how a sex-linked gene for intellectual growth could result in greater male variability, let us assume that there are only six variants (alleles) of the neotenous gene, each resulting in a different rate and duration of intellectual growth. The least effective of these alleles would result in a very limited growth, what amounts to mental deficiency. The most effective would lead to maximum mental growth, with the other alleles intermediate in effect, in proportion to their numerical position on figure 15-1. That is, the allele for "6" would result in greater growth than that for "5", which would be greater than for "4", and so on.

Let us further assume that these alleles occur in the population with a frequency distribution similar to the expansion of the binomial, in the proportions 1 : 5 : 10 : 10 : 5 : 1, with the middle values of growth the most frequent. This is not unrealistic, although it is undoubtedly greatly simplified. We know that most new mutations are unfavorable, but most of these are eventually eliminated by natural selection. Highly favorable mutations would be relatively rare, but they would tend to remain in the population and even increase over the generations, as a result of natural selection. However, over short evolutionary distances the most frequent alleles would be those for the middle levels.

For this X-linked trait, the number of males at each level of final mental growth would be the same as the gene frequency, barring a few cases where events such as disease, trauma or genetic disorders involving the brain reduced the intellectual level. The theoretical distribution for 1024 males is shown in figure 15-1.

For females, however, the level of functioning would depend on the average of two alleles, according to the Lyon hypothesis. Thus, for a female to function at the lowest level it would be necessary for her to have inherited allele No. 1 from both parents. Since that allele has a theoretical frequency of 1 in 32, the chance of a female inheriting the same defective gene from *both* parents is 1 in 32^2 or one in 1024, assuming no selective mating. The same would apply to allele No. 6, at the high end of the scale.

At the same time, average values would be more common for females, since a low value on one X-chromosome would probably be offset by a higher value on the other. The same effect, basically regression to the mean, would be expected for unusually high values. The distribution that would be expected for 1024 females, on the same baseline as for males, is shown in figure 15-2.

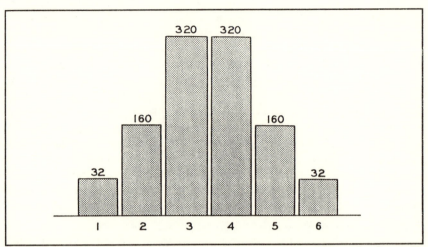

Figure 15-1. Hypothetical distribution of phenotypes among 1024 males for an X-linked recessive gene with six alleles.

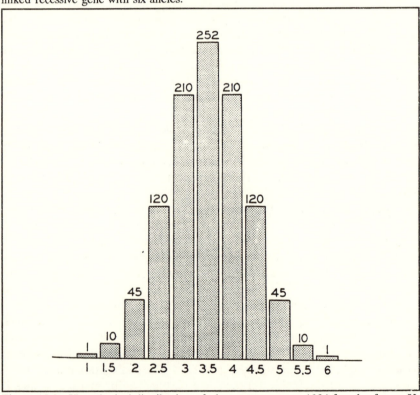

Figure 15-2. Hypothetical distribution of phenotypes among 1024 females for an X-linked recessive gene with six alleles.

144

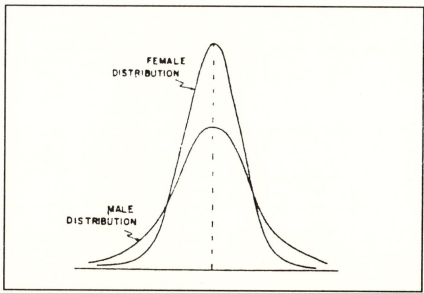

Figure 15-3. Distributions from figures 15-1 and 15-2 superimposed and expressed as curves.

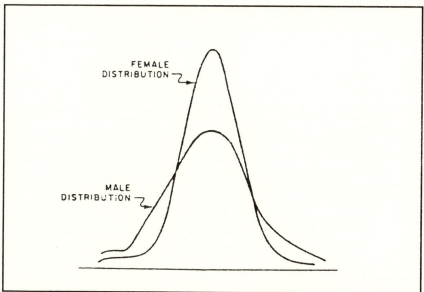

Figure 15-4. Probable distributions of IQ in the population, by sex, with differences exaggerated for clarity.

When the results are presented as superimposed curves, as in figure 15-3, it is apparent that there is a greater variance for males than females. However, because more males are affected by physiological conditions resulting in severe mental defect, and also are more likely to be marginal or subnormal in intelligence because of X-linked factors, the distributions shown in figure 15-4 are more accurate, and when combined, correspond closely to the distribution of IQs previously shown in figure 12-7, B.

Male : Female Ratios at Various Levels of IQ

The evidence cited above makes a strong case for greater male variability in intelligence. Data from Jensen (1971) and others cited earlier in this chapter shows that on an average females are somewhat brighter than males. What does this tell us about the comparative intellectual abilities of males and females?

If males are simply more variable in IQ than females, and if that greater variability applies to both ends of the scale, it should be possible to estimate the male : female ratios above or below any given level. However, when plotted (figure 15-5), even using the lowest of the estimates of differences

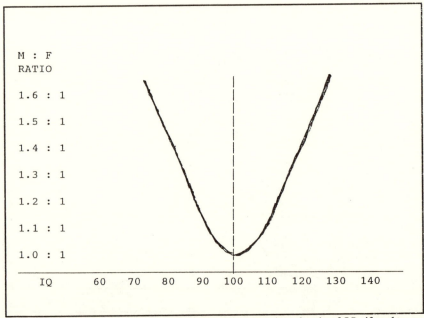

Figure 15-5. Approximate male : female ratios at various levels of IQ, if males are 13 percent more variable.

in variance previously cited (Roberts, Norman, and Griffiths, 1945), the relative numbers of males at the high end of the scale becomes excessive, with about 60 percent more males than females with IQs over 130. That discrepancy would be even greater using the higher (and probably more realistic) figures from the other studies cited in chapter 14. The best empirical data available (see chapter 14) give a figure if less than 40 percent. Thus the hypothesis of greater male variability in intellectual ability cannot, per se, account for the differences between the sexes that exist.

Another hypothesis, suggested by Jensen's (1971) data, is that females average a point higher than males in mean IQ. The resulting ratios are shown in figure 15-6. That hypothesis puts the sex ratios in the ballpark at the low end of the scale, but it would also result in a female excess at IQs above 130. Since that doesn't square with available data, the hypothesis that a higher mean IQ for females accounts for the differences must be abandoned.

However, The X-linkage theory also implies that males are more variable in intelligence test scores. So, what if we chart male : female ratios, using an assumption that females have a mean IQ of 100.5 compared with 99.5 for males; and at the same time their standard deviation is 14.5 compared to the

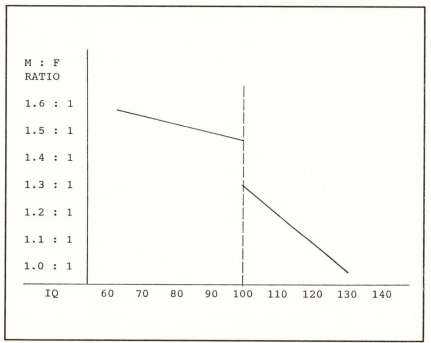

Figure 15-6. Approximate male : female ratios at various levels of IQ, if females are 1 point higher in mean IQ.

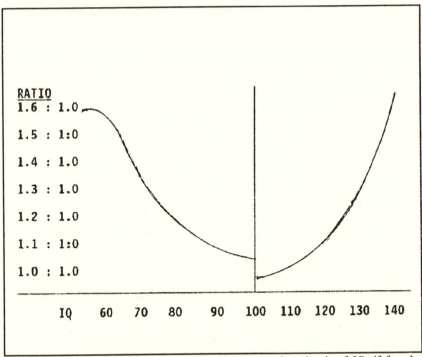

Figure 15-7. Approximate male : female ratios at various levels of IQ, if females have a 1-point higher mean IQ and males have a 13 percent greater standard deviation.

males' 15.5? That's about a 7 percent greater variance for males, less than the differences shown in the epidemiological data in the previous chapter but not too far out of line.

Then we get a pattern something like that shown in figure 15-7, which agrees essentially with the epidemiological and survey data. The decrease in ratios at the low end of the scale is due to the presence of "single-event" cases of mental subnormality, such as Down's syndrome and other clinical types. The prevalence of most such disorders would be expected to be about the same for both sexes.

It should be understood that male-female differences at the high and low ends of the scale involve very few people. For instance, only about 3 or 4 persons in a thousand would be expected to have IQs over 140, although this might be increased slightly by occasional new mutations.

Then we get a pattern something like that shown in figure 15-7, which agrees essentially with the epidemiological and survey data. The decrease in ratios at the low end of the scale is due to the presence of "single-event" cases of mental subnormality, such as Down's syndrome and other clinical types. The prevalence of most such disorders would be expected to be about the same for both sexes.

To summarize, if males have a mean IQ of 99.5 and females, of 100.5; and males a standard deviation of 15.5 compared with 14.5 for females, the expected proportion of males to females would be:

Below IQ 70	67 percent more males
Below IQ 85	21 percent more males
Below IQ 100	1 percent more males
Above IQ 115	equal numbers
Above IQ 130	14 percent more males
Above IQ 135	33 percent more males
Above IQ 140	67 percent more males

While these figures are only approximate, it is apparent that a model based on greater male variability *and* higher female mean IQ provides the best fit for available data.

When High Levels of Several Abilities Are Required

The effect of greater male variability would be even more pronounced when two or more X-linked intellectual capacities are involved. For instance, vocations requiring a combination of high-level verbal-cognitive, mathematical, and spatial abilities, such as some fields of engineering, would end up as the almost-exclusive domain of men. That is a situation that has long existed.

Male Chauvinism?

Without denying that females of exceptionally high intelligence exist in large numbers, it is not at all unlikely that there are even greater numbers of male geniuses. Thus, the excess of men in positions requiring the very highest levels of intellectual or technical capability would be more a consequence of genetic factors than of male chauvinism.

Still, Samuel Johnson put it most succinctly over 200 years ago. When asked which were more intelligent, men or women, he replied, "Which man? Which woman?"

Chapter 16

Editorial Comment: What Good Is All This?

> The perpetual skeptic asked the scientist, "What good is your discovery? It has no practical use." The scientist replied, "What good is a new-born baby?"

The theories, and the facts to back them up, have been presented, and now the author turns from his task as a scientist and becomes philosophical. The professional in search of data, the professor in search of a new point of view for his or her course, the legislator or member of the judiciary—all these can stop here, if they wish. But if they do go on, they are likely to find that this last chapter is disturbing. So be it.

In the first chapter of this book, there was a quotation from the introduction to Will Durant's (1943, p. 2) book, *The Story of Philosophy*, that deserves to be repeated here, but at greater length.

> We can be sure that if we find wisdom, all things else will be added to us. "Seek ye first the good things of the mind," Bacon admonishes us, "and the rest will either be supplied or its loss will not be felt". Truth will not make us rich, but it will make us free.
>
> Some ungentle reader will check us here by informing us that philosophy is as useless as chess, as obscure as ignorance, and as stagnant as content. "There is nothing so absurd," said Cicero, "but that it may be found in the books of the philosophers". Doubtless some philosophers have had all sorts of wisdom except common sense; and many a philosophic flight has been due to the elevating power of thin air. . . . But is philosophy stagnant? Science seems always to advance, while philosophy seems always to lose ground. Yet this is only because philosophy accepts the hard and hazardous task of dealing with problems not yet open to the methods of science.

Virtually all of us strongly defend our philosophical underpinnings, generally derived from our parents, colleagues, and social background, as the one true source of all wisdom. In so doing, we forget, or ignore, the fact that others equally as competent as ourselves may not share our philosophy. Thence is the source of all sorts of conflict, which generally is resolved only slowly, even in the light of new knowledge. Or else, the situation is resolved by repression or warfare.

Many of us cling to concepts that were taught to us in our earlier years, including our college days, without looking at them objectively when new ideas or new facts arise. As a result, our thinking becomes outdated and we continue to deal with the problems that face us as ineffectively as ever. And we don't even realize it!

A positive commitment to a particular philosophy, or group of philosophies, has some definite advantages. It makes it easier to make decisions. It also lends a degree of assurance to one's attitudes, an element of self-confidence, that is often contagious. The blatherings of an evangelist, or a hidebound teacher, who has no apparent doubt about his or her eternal rightness, can convince even some fairly strong-minded individuals.

However, as philosopher Will Durant suggested, there are other means of making decisions than purely philosophical ones, providing one has the necessary knowledge. In the long run, decisions based on intelligent interpretation of actual facts, what might be called scientific decisions, are more likely to work, and to the benefit of more people. They may, of course, cause temporary disruptions, or even severely inconvenience a minority of individuals or groups. Or, for all too many people, they may lead to disturbing doubts about one's basic philosophies.

The first step in solving a question that has not already been adequately answered is to gather data. Modern-day scientists are great at that.

For the simpler questions that face us, gathering data is often enough. Given adequate information, a person or group often can work out a solution. However, seeking out more knowledge can also be a means of delaying or avoiding a decision. For instance, rather than taking a positive action that is sure to offend a lot of voters, our legislative bodies procrastinate by appointing a committee or two to study the matter further.

Even having data at hand, however, isn't always helpful in those cases where a decision must be made. We may know a lot of facts, but they either don't make sense or they are misinterpreted, often because of the biases of the persons doing the interpreting.

A classic example of that latter outcome has already been discussed in chapter 13, that is, the Supreme Court decision to integrate schools. The data were there in abundance; the (presumably) great minds of the justices wrestled with the question, with the assistance of a person (Dr. Coleman) who had delved deeply into the matter. A decision was made, and at great inconvenience to the schools, and even more to the students, busing to integrate schools was instituted. The only problem was, and still is, that it didn't work. Black students, on an average, still do not do as well as Caucasian and Oriental students, and hundreds of thousands of young people waste time riding in buses when they could be in the classroom or in other more rewarding occupations. If anything, the "solution" made matters worse.

As was previously mentioned, Dr. Coleman later recognized that he had misinterpreted his data. Still, integration of schools has become a philosophical credo as well as a law, and integration (even against the wishes of students and their parents in many cases) remains a rule.

In that case, as in many others, a *theory* was needed to fit the facts together into a meaningful whole, to help the scientists and the Court see the relationships among the items of data. Unfortunately, in that particular case, the theory that was tried was based more on the idealistic philosophies of its proponents (and indeed of almost everyone) than on a critical appraisal of all of the available knowledge. By the time the primary proponent of integration, Dr. Coleman, gained the maturity and deeper knowledge to look more objectively at his own conclusions, the Supreme Court had already made its decision. (For more details, go back to chapter 13.) Generally, though, an *objectively* derived theory is far better than no theory at all when it comes to interpreting complex sets of data.

Philosophies and customs do make possible quick and easy decisions. Without such crutches the process of making *personal* decisions would slow us down intolerably. However, when there is time for consideration, and especially when other people are involved, logic rather than preset responses should prevail.

The author must admit that some ideas that seem logically sound do not agree with his own personal and philosophical feelings. But over all, the scientific ideas are preferable in a broad social sense.

For instance, it is all well and good to have the philosophy that "all Men are created equal." However, we must look into the meaning of this statement. First of all, it is a *moral*, or philosophical, principle, not a scientific one. In a *moral* sense, everyone has the same status.

Secondly, being "equal" does not mean that everyone is the same. And yet, all too often we make the assumption that other people do, or should, have the same value system and abilities as we do.

On the basis of the misinterpreted philosophy of equality we assume that because formal education beyond the basics has been important in our own lives that the same is, or should be, true for everyone else. American educational systems all too often continue to be elitist, trying to educate everyone along the same lines as those followed by the teachers and school officials, even though more and more students are unable either to assimilate or to benefit, now or later, from much of what is taught.

I do not mean to infer that in an increasingly complex society more education is not necessary for many, if not most, students. And, if nothing else, school provides a supervised situation that permits the mother (who may be the only parent) to work and support or help support her family. However, it is logical that greater efforts must be made to make education *meaningful* to every student, not just to those who are average or above in learning capacity. That means, among other things, adjusting the rate of teaching to the capacities of the individual student and providing those students who are slower in maturation with additional time to reach the level of readiness needed to develop necessary skills. It means, also, a deemphasis on performance testing as a means of evaluating a school system, a school, or a teacher, however useful it may be in evaluating individual students.

Trying to cram fourth-grade reading down the throat of a child not ready for it, or Shakespeare into the mind of a student who is barely up to Sam Spade, is not only futile, it is cruel and destructive of motivation. Unlike those in Denmark and many other countries, few United States schools offer an adequate curriculum for students whose goals do not include higher education.

The relative lack of consideration of individual students' needs can be the source of many problems. For instance, as mentioned in chapter 15, according to one study there were about 75 percent more boys than girls in high school level special education classes in the U.S. However, studies at the high end of the scale do not show anywhere near that level of excess of males, except possibly at stratospheric levels of IQ. The so-called normal curve would seem to be skewed in that there are many more mentally disabled males than very bright ones. However, that excess probably isn't due only to differences in intelligence, per se, but also to several other X-linked factors, including deficits in spatial perception (reading disability and some cases of arithmetic disability), as well as environmental factors that interact with and amplify genetic differences.

In effect, the reason for the excess of males with learning problems could be that more boys than girls start out with X-linked problems (slower rate of intellectual development, plus reading and arithmetic disorders associated with under-developed spatial perception, and the like) that leave them behind academically. Classroom teaching continues at the rate determined by the average and above-average students and by administratively established curricula, and more boys than girls get left in the lurch. The cases of Ricky and Jim, mentioned in chapter 13, show how such an interaction between educational and environmental factors can work.

With the aid of exceptional teachers, a few such boys go on to satisfactory completion of school. However, although today's teachers are, for the most part, better trained than those of even a generation ago, the really exceptional qualities needed for dealing with those students who do not fit the usual pattern are relatively rare. This is made worse by the tendency for teaching programs to be imposed from the top and by demands made of individual schools and teachers that their students produce test scores above some state or national average, without regard to the nature or needs of the students. In too many cases, school administrators look at the test results as scores in a competition, without regard to what they tell about the students, in order to promote what Sowell (1993) calls "institutional image".

On the other hand, as Herrnstein and Murray (1994) point out, the tendency to "dumb down" school work should be done in such a way as not to have a negative effect on the college preparatory courses. Here again is a situation where integrated schools may have a deleterious effect, by diluting the curricula on behalf of the lower-functioning students.

Importance of the X-linkage Theory to Science

An unfortunate side effect of the theory of X-linkage of major intellectual traits is that almost all previous research regarding the heritability of such traits must be reexamined. It is highly probable that all present estimates of the heritability of intelligence are too low because father-son correlations were not excluded from the analyses. Under the X-linkage theory, most father-son correlations should be a function of father-mother correlations, without any substantial *direct* genetic basis.

X-Linkage Theory and Legislative and Judicial Decision Making

While the importance of sex differences in the distribution of intellectual abilities may be more obvious when it comes to professional employment in ivied-wall settings, it is no less true in other areas involving intellectual capacities. It can do much more harm than good to pass laws and promote court rulings that group differences in the distribution of intellectual abilities do not exist. Legislative bodies cannot enact new laws of nature, nor can courts overturn them, and attempts to do so lead to decreased social and economic productivity over all.

X-Linkage Theory and Social and Welfare Programs

While it may offend our democratic senses, it is about time to recognize that a substantial part of our population growth comes from mothers (not families) who are intellectually subaverage. Because the mother passes on her genes for intelligence to all of her children, and the father only to the girls, females have twice as much effect on the intellectual capabilities of future generations as do males.

For all too many girls and women, the only licit career that fits their intellectual and educational abilities is motherhood, not infrequently at the expense of the taxpayer. Not only are a great many of these women unfit in the sense of providing proper care and motivation to their children, they pass on X-chromosomes with marginal or deficient instructions for the intellectual development of their offspring. And these offspring, in turn, breed another generation of morons, to use a harsh word.

There was a time when our country could use a plentiful supply of strong backs and people willing to perform tedious, repetitive labor requiring only limited intellectual capabilities. There still is some demand for such, now often filled by immigrant labor from Mexico or Puerto Rico. While some of the persons from our own urban and rural slums are willing to accept menial or physical labor as a source of livelihood, all too many of them turn to crime (or welfare motherhood) as a source of income and to sex and drugs as sources of personal fulfillment. Consequently, their economic and social output is negative rather than positive.

The deterioration of overall intelligence is happening at a time when there is less and less room for persons of limited intellectual capabilities in our society. The computer, more than any invention of recent years, has created a schism of employability. A greater and greater proportion of present-day jobs demand an intellectual level above the 50th percentile in our present population.

It is therefore extremely important that we start to take into account the uncontrolled breeding of persons with inferior levels of intelligence. It isn't only in the workplace that higher intelligence is becoming necessary. The very skills needed for maintaining a functioning democracy are being threatened by the large numbers of persons who are unable to participate intelligently in our government processes, including elections.

It may be sad for liberals to contemplate, but the day is approaching when *reproductive rights* will have to be licensed and controlled. That's nothing new, of course. Marriage licenses, as a means of controlling marriages and reproduction, have been a part of our culture for many generations, although liberalized laws in many states have made them less and less useful in preventing the birth of defective and subnormal children. Now, however, an increasingly large proportion of all births occurs outside of marriage and thus even the weak marriage licensing laws have no effect.

As an aside, this author has no objections to marital or even nonmarital sexual relationships involving persons who are limited in their intellectual capabilities, provided that no children result. He has been the advocate and/or counsellor in at least eight marriages in which both parents were subnormal. However, in every case the necessary steps were taken to see that there would be no offspring. This was primarily for the benefit of society as a whole because, as Reed and Reed (1965) pointed out, the risk of mental defect for each child in such marriages is about 40 percent. In some of the cases, the actual genetic risk was greater than 50 percent. But it was also out of consideration for the couple involved, since the demands of child rearing were well beyond them. Living together as a couple was about the limit of their capabilities.

Almost as important as the social problems created by an increasingly large population of persons of limited intellect are those caused by the smaller number of clinically identifiable mental subnormals. It has already been mentioned that much of such subnormality is X-linked. If one adds to the category of "mental subnormality" borderline mental retardation and learning disorders, the proportion of mental defect linked to genes on the X-chromosome could easily exceed 90 percent! In effect, X-linked genes are the "familial" basis for what is still called "cultural-familial mental deficiency" and the major cause of less severe intellectual deficits and learning disorders.

In addition, the implication that males are more variable in intelligence than females, at both ends of the scale, should be taken into account in legislative, administrative, and judicial decisions regarding women's rights issues. As previously mentioned, Congress can pass no new laws of nature, nor can the courts overturn those laws. "Affirmative action," the preferential hiring or promotion of people simply on the basis of race or sex, can only lower the efficiency of the work force, and this affects all of us.

X-Linkage Theory and Education

The theory of X-linkage of major intellectual traits and its corollary, the genetic control of patterns of intellectual growth, affect our educational system from first grade through graduate school. The patterns of teaching in the earliest grades, even the age of admitting children to school, should certainly be looked at. So should the schools' preoccupation with preparing all children for higher education. However, that does not imply "dumbing down" classes for above-average students.

Another factor must be taken into account. As previously mentioned, it is highly probable that memory, as an intellectual trait, is *not* X-linked. Thus, it is important to differentiate between "learning" and "intelligence." In older times, learning was highly respected, since very few people were in a position to acquire higher levels of education. By *learning* the traditions and prejudices of the predominant group, based on the prevalent philosophy, priests and teachers could come up with doctrines and decisions that were acceptable in a less sophisticated world. However, in the modern world, that is not always true. Having a huge stock of lore or knowledge from which to make decisions may be relatively less useful than in more primitive times, and can often sidetrack the search for new knowledge. The ideal situation combines knowledge with the ability to evaluate that knowledge, and then to select and reconfigure it into new discoveries. Knowledge might be compared to raw materials; and intelligence, to the tools by which knowledge is manipulated.

Good teaching, especially at the college level, should involve more than the passing on of facts. It should also encourage critical and creative thinking, but it certainly should not involve philosophical proselyting.

Intelligence and Learning

Because people of higher intelligence are better able to organize their learning, and to make it meaningful, they tend to learn faster and more than those with less intelligence. Consequently, there is a tendency to confuse learning and intelligence. There are many interactions between the two, but it must be understood that they are not the same. For one thing, there seems to be no evidence that the ability to learn, as a separate ability, is an X-linked characteristic, although actual research is lacking. As previously mentioned, the basic ability to learn from experience and training was probably not greatly enhanced by the Adam mutation.

If the author happened to be a professor trying to demonstrate the relationship between intelligence and learning, he would probably present the following problem to the class:

> There is a company that turns out as its only product ornamental concrete statues, which it sells for $29 each. Professional gardeners buy them in large quantities for their clients. To get them, the gardeners take their trucks to a storage lot where a husky but not-too-bright man helps them load and presents them with a bill. One day one of these gardeners came in and bought 31 of the statues. How much was his bill?

Most of the students would take paper and pencil and work out the problem as follows:

$$
\begin{array}{r}
31 \\
\times\ 29 \\
\hline
279 \\
62 \\
\hline
899
\end{array}
$$

A few would simplify the arithmetic a little by putting the "31" on the bottom line, so that they could multiply by 1, as follows:

$$
\begin{array}{r}
29 \\
\times\ 31 \\
\hline
29 \\
87 \\
\hline
899
\end{array}
$$

A very bright student or two (who happened to have had a course in algebra) would recognize a familiar pattern. Such a student would note that the problem could be expressed, "(30 + 1) X (30 - 1)". In other words, "(X+1)(X-1)" which equals "X^2-1". Then, 30^2-1 = 899 would lead to the same result as that obtained more laboriously by arithmetic. So who came up with the answer in the shortest time?

The answer? The employee at the statuary yard! After months or years on the job he knew, without even looking it up on the chart in the office, what the price for 31 statues would be.

In effect, learning provides the quickest and most reliable response to most situations the average person faces. The ability to learn by rote varies far less than intelligence between individuals. When I worked at a state institution, I knew a mentally subnormal man who could quote extensively from the dictionary, including definitions of unusual words, but he hadn't a clue as to what the definitions meant!

A person may be extremely well learned, but not very bright. I know of a few professors whose knowledge of their subject is incredible but who have only limited ability to make intelligent inferences from that knowledge. Cognitive ability, or IQ in its popular sense, can be a definite asset when one holds a job requiring meeting new challenges and making original decisions; but, at the same time, it sometimes leads to boredom and carelessness in jobs that are highly repetitive.

Once upon a time, mere learning was highly respected because so few people had access to higher education. However, this respect often led to difficulties. The opinions of the old-time minister of the gospel, who had had at least a modicum of higher education, were accepted even when they were downright stupid, and that sometimes resulted in personal problems for the parishioners. Even today, people who rely too greatly on previous learning, without evaluating its appropriateness to the current situation, can create problems for themselves and others.

Because they are able to make knowledge meaningful—to organize what they learn—persons with high intelligence tend to be able to acquire and retain more knowledge. As a result, there is a tendency to confuse learning with intelligence. Moreover, in many situations, mere knowledge plus a modicum of intelligence is usually enough, providing there is someone to turn to when something unusual comes up. One advantage an intelligent person has is that he or she is more able to determine when a rote solution is appropriate, and to figure out an alternative track when it isn't.

On the job, a problem is likely to arise when the person does his or her work so well by sheer rote that he or she is promoted to the position of being the one others must turn to with problems. (I believe that's one basis for the so-called "Peter Principle", which states that a person rises to his or her level of incompetence).

In our society, unlike the more primitive ones of the past and in most of the third-world countries today, many of the skills needed in later life are taught in school. When these skills are not learned, the person has limited capabilities for economic and personal development. The point is near when there will be fewer and fewer opportunities for persons without basic literacy and numerical skills. Nowadays, computer skills are becoming another necessity.

While our schools do a good job with those students who are average or above in intelligence, they seem to be failing miserably in meeting the needs of those whose developmental schedule is slow. While there are certainly individual teachers who work seeming miracles with slow students, mainly by giving them a new start toward basic skills learning when they are ready for it, they are still greatly in the minority.

Perhaps the answer is competency-based, as opposed to age-based, advancement in school classes. There are, in fact, schools that work on that basis and which are reported to be remarkably successful. And even today, there is a widely advertised home study course in phonics that is being marketed, mainly (it seems) for persons who were not physically and mentally ready to learn that reading technique when they were in first and second grade and who just need another shot at the subject after they are physically and intellectually mature.

This should not be taken as an endorsement of phonics as a cure-all for literacy problems. The person who relies on sounding out words (the phonics approach) often ends up being a slow reader who can be handicapped in keeping up with the demands of his or her job unless he or she learns a more efficient approach to reading. But at least he or she can read.

One of my own past employers (Honeywell) actually hired a speed-reading instructor to help supervisors, foremen, engineers and others to overcome their tendency to silently pronounce the words they read. They were of the generation when phonics was the sole approach to reading. However, the time it took such employees to go through the paper work on their desks kept them away from the other aspects of their jobs. The speed-reading instructor was very successful, at least on a temporary basis, in getting the students to use rapid scanning techniques, involving whole-word recognition.

The students learned to read a word or a group of words at a time, not a syllable at a time.

In any case, it is likely that competency-based education could salvage many of the increasing numbers of low-IQ persons for more productive lives. It would not increase their intelligence, per se, although due to the nature of most intelligence tests, it might well increase their IQs to some extent. What it would improve is their educational level. That is just one implication of the theory that X-linked genes control a *growth pattern* rather than some final result.

It is apparent that above-average IQ is not essential for *basic* academic learning, although it certainly makes it easier. Where exceptionally high intelligence is almost essential is in making the new discoveries that permit society to advance. Without the small number of people at the top of the intellectual scale, including the inventors, the discoverers, and the theoreticians, humanity could still be living a life only a little more advanced than rather bright apes.

The civilized world needs to have a substantial proportion of its population in the "very bright" range just to maintain our civilization at its present level. To continue to make progress, it needs a goodly number of those who are truly brilliant, whose genius should not be stifled or sidetracked by mercenary concerns.

Most important of all, there is compelling evidence that, at least in the United States, there is a continuing decline in national intelligence that has already resulted in lowered economic power and productivity (Itzkoff, 1994). In fact, on a world-wide scale, Itzkoff (1992) contends that such social evils as poverty, social pathology and human degradation are largely due to low human intelligence and the resulting inability to compete in highly complex social and economic environments.

In Summary

As Gerd Gigerenzer, Director of the Center for Adaptive Behavior and Cognition of the Max Planck Institute for Psychological Research, said, "Much of psychology now consists of vague theories that don't spell out precise predictions. Productive theories about the mind will have to risk being precise and opening themselves up to being disproved." (Quoted in Bower, 1996a, p. 25).

Since its purpose is to present just such precise theories, along with a few of the hypotheses that can be derived therefrom, this book is not intended to supply new data, nor to provide more than a partial summary of what information is available. Its goal is simply to provide an organized theory of human intelligence, which is open to further proof, or possibly, disproof.

Scientific (not philosophical) evaluation of the theories can provide an efficient method for gaining an understanding of higher human mental processes. In some cases, such as the educational methods just discussed, the theoretical approach may lead to improvements in the techniques used to deal with problems that have long existed.

But, don't look for any dramatic changes overnight. As Max Planck, the noted physicist, once said, "A new scientific truth does not triumph by convincing its opponents and making them see the light, but rather because its opponents eventually die, and a new generation grows up that is familiar with it" (Planck, 1949).

Glossary

* indicates a cross reference.

allele. An alternative form of a gene or Mendelian characteristic. For instance, the genes for the melanic and "wild-type" coloration of the moth *Biston betularia*, as described in chapter 9, are allelic.

amino acids. Organic acids containing the amino group, NH_2 They can be assembled genetically into proteins*.

aneuploidy. The situation that exists when there is extra or missing chromosomal material in a set.

assortative mating. The tendency for like to mate with like.

autosome. A chromosome* other than a sex chromosome. A normal human has 22 pairs of autosomes.

axons. The cell fibers that conduct nerve impulses away from the cell body. They are usually longer than the dendrites*.

bar-eye. A mutation caused by the doubling* of a section of the X-chromosome* in fruit flies. It results in an oval rather than round conformation of the eye. (See also double-bar*.)

Barr body. A small object within the nucleus of somatic cells in females. It is, in effect, the "turned-off" second X-chromosome*.

borderline. A term used to describe individuals who are intellectually dull but not quite subnormal. The intelligence test scores of borderline individuals would ordinarily range from 71 to 85. This meaning should not be confused with the psychiatric term "borderline," which refers to a personality pattern rather than to intellectual ability.

chromosome. A filament composed of genetic material, along which genetic instructions are located. In humans there are 46 such chromosomes in 23 half-sets, one such half-set from each parent. They are found in the nuclei of most cells in the body.

cognitive ability. The ability to use higher mental processes such as comprehension of abstract concepts, logic, and planning.

controlling gene. A gene or group of genes controlling the operation of one or more structural genes.

Cro-Magnon Man. A strain of early Man that has been generally been considered to be the ancestral stock of *Homo sapiens**. The first Cro-Magnon remains discovered, now known to date back about 35,000 years, were found in substantial numbers in southwest central France, particularly around the town of Les Eyzies.

crossing over. A process during meiosis* in which corresponding parts of paternally and maternally derived chromosomes* intermix, thus providing greater genetic variability.

cytoplasm. The material, including fluid, organelles, and various membranes, that occurs between the outer cell wall and the nucleus of a cell. These organelles include the mitochondria*.

deletion. An area on a chromosome* from which some genetic material has been lost.

dendrites. The branches of a nerve cell that transmit impulses toward the body of the cell. See also axons*.

DNA. The "coding" element of chromosomes*.

dominant gene. A gene that results in a certain phenotype*, even in the presence of an allele* that codes for a different phenotype. The dominant "wild-type" gene for light coloration of *Biston betularia* predominates even in the presence of the other gene for darker coloration on the other allele (see chapter 9). However, it is not uncommon that the effect of the dominant gene is slightly modified by the recessive gene in hetero-zygotes*.

dominant half of the brain. The half of the brain, usually the side opposite the dominant hand, that includes the centers for logic, reasoning, and language.

double-bar. A mutation caused by the further doubling of a section of the X-chromosome* in fruit flies. It results in an eye that is even narrower than that associated with the single doubling. (See also bar-eye*.)

doubling or **duplication (chromosome)**. The replication of a section of a chromosome*, usually found within that same chromosome and ordinari-ly adjacent to the original portion. The duplicated section may end up having no identifiable function or with an entirely different function from the original.

eukaryotic cells. See nucleated cells.

founder effect. The tendency for genetic characteristics of the aboriginals of a group to persist in future generations.

fragile-X syndrome. A condition, found only in laboratory studies, in which X-chromosomes* fragment when they go through mitosis in a nutrient-deficient culture medium. When the sample in which such fragile X-chromosomes are found is grown from a male's cells, that male is virtual-ly always mentally subnormal*, autistic, or the victim of learning disabili-ties. Females with the fragile X would be carriers of the fragile-X syn-drome.

***g*-factor** (or **general factor**). A general factor found by Spearman to underlie many types of intelligence test scores. Factors for certain special abilities have also been identified.

gamete. A mature male or female reproductive cell in higher forms of life, for instance, sperm (or pollen) and ova. Such cells contain only a hap-loid set of chromosomes*, so that when they combine with another ga-mete of the opposite type, a full chromosome complement again exists.

genetic lethal. A genetic condition that reduces the likelihood of reproduc-tion of the carrier. It need not be lethal in a literal sense, although it sometimes is. Tay-Sachs disease, which causes early death of infants, is lethal in both senses. Achondroplasia which permits a normal life span, but tends to reduce the suitability of its victims as mates, is a lethal only in the genetic sense.

genotype. The characteristics that an individual inherits and can pass on to his or her offspring. See phenotype*.

heterozygous. Having two different alleles* at a gene locus. For instance, some specimens of *Biston betularia* (see chapter 9) carry both the gene for the dominant, or wild-type, coloration and that for melanism.

Homo erectus. Modern Man's most recent ancestor. Adam's peers were *Homo erectus*. Adam was the first *Homo sapiens**, having inherited the gene or genes for higher intelligence from his mother.

Homo sapiens. The species that is modern Man, Adam's descendants who inherited the gene for higher intelligence from him through his daughters and their descendants.

homozygous. Having inherited the same gene at a given locus from both parents.

hypothesis. A *testable* presumption based on existing data.

idiot. A now obsolete term for a person with the most severe level of mental subnormality, with an IQ below 30 or so.

idiot savant. Persons of subnormal intellectual functioning who display some exceptional talent. For example, they may be capable of doing remarkable feats of mental arithmetic, determine the day of the week for a particular date without resorting to a calendar, or have exceptional musical ability.

imbecile. A now obsolete term for a person in the middle range of mental subnormality*, with an IQ of 30 to 50 or thereabout.

insertion. A bit of chromosomal material inserted into a chromosome*. In at least some cases the inserted material, regardless of its origin, acts as a controlling gene*.

inversion. A condition in which a group of genes is inverted in respect to the norm for that chromosome*. Generally, inversions do not prevent a chromosome from being involved in reproduction, nor do they always result in identifiable abnormalities of the phenotype*, since the chromosomes can still pair up by means of loop formation. However, errors in chromosomal matching-up due to loop formation can result in muta tions*.

Lamarckian theory of evolution. A pre-Darwinian theory of evolution, going back to the work of Jean Baptiste Lamarck (1744-1829). The theory was, for example, that giraffes developed their long necks by stretching them to reach leaves on trees, and that these changes were somehow passed on to the next generation, which continued the process.

learning disorder. A learning problem more circumscribed than mental retardation* or mental subnormality*. In some cases it is limited to some skill, such as the ability to read or to do arithmetic.

left brain. The half of the brain involved with cognitive abilities and speech. In most right-handed people, it is on the left side, whence the name.

Martin-Bell syndrome. An eponym for non-specific X-linked mental subnormality. (See non-specific mental retardation*; X-linked mental subnormality*.)

mathematical ability. The ability to do advanced mathematical reasoning, as differentiated from the ability to do simple calculations.

maturation. The process by which physical and mental growth proceed to a point of readiness for particular tasks, such as reading, the understanding of concepts, etc. The rate of maturation for a given process can vary greatly between individuals and, on an average, between groups.

meiosis. The process of forming the chromosomal bases for sperm or ova. In the process, full sets of chromosomes* are reduced to haploid sets to create gametes* (ova or sperm cells). In humans, the haploid set includes one of each of the 22 autosomes* plus an X- or Y-chromosome*.

Mendelian. Following the basic rules of genetics as set forth by Gregor Mendel, the founder of the science.

mental deficiency. Intellectual defect of a permanent nature that seriously affects the individual's social, educational and economic functioning. In this book, the term is *not* synonymous with mental retardation*.

mental retardation. Slower than average maturation* of intelligence, or of school readiness. While usually associated with low cognitive ability, many of the associated problems will sometimes disappear with time as maturation* increases relative to others of the same chronological age. In such cases the residual problems may be more a matter of educational deficit than of inadequate intelligence.

mental subnormality. An alternative term for mental deficiency*.

mitochondria. Minute organelles found in all except the most primitive cells. They work as metabolizers to provide the energy by which the cell functions. An interesting characteristic is that they are, in themselves, separate living organisms, having their own genetic material and reproducing separately from the cell within which they are located. Another interesting characteristic is that they are transmitted from generation to generation through the cytoplasm*. Therefore, all transmission of the genes for the mitochondria in humans, as in other higher life forms, plant and animal, is through the female line since, because, unlike the ova (egg cells), male sex cells have no cytoplasm.

mitosis. The process by which the chromosome* set in the nucleus of a cell divides itself up so as to provide the genetic basis for another cell.

molecular disease. A term used by Linus Pauling to designate disorders resulting from chromosomal mutations*. These include a wide range of genetic conditions, from achondroplasia to xeroderma. Dr. Pauling also seemed to hint that exceptionally superior intelligence relative to the surrounding population is such a disorder.

moron. An obsolete term for a person in the upper range of mental subnormality*, with an IQ roughly in the range of 50 to 70.

mosaicism. A situation in which some body cells, or clumps of body cells, carry a certain genetic trait and others a different one. This is a common occurrence. For instance, persons with blood type AB are a mosaic for blood types A and B.

musical ability. A capability of understanding and utilizing the elements of music that goes beyond mere performance.

mutation. A change in the genetic instructions for an organism. Often this change would also involve the gametes*, so it could be passed on to at least some of the offspring.

natural selection. The phenomenon of some individuals being genetically better fitted to survive than others, and therefore being better able to reproduce and pass on their genes to future generations.

Neanderthal Man. The original "Neanderthal Man" was a skull found in the Neander area of Germany in 1856. It was not recognized at the time as a predecessor of modern Man, since at the time the Biblical version of Adam held sway, and it was assumed that species were immutable. That is, Man, and other creatures as well, was created in the form that existed at the time.

neoteny. The retention of an early developmental phenotype for a longer period than is usual for a type of organism. An example is the down found on newly hatched birds which as the result of a neotenous muta-tion* (or series of neotenous mutations) remains throughout life in pen-guins.

non-specific mental subnormality or **non-specific mental retardation**. Men-tal subnormality* that has no known physiological basis outside of the central nervous system. It presumably results from a developmental de-fect, probably due to a remutation of the genes controlling intellectual development. In the medical literature particularly, such subnormality is often identified by the eponyms Martin-Bell syndrome* or Renpenning syndrome*.

nucleated (eukaryotic) cells. Cells containing a nucleus with genetic material in the form of chromosomes*. By contrast, in simple cells, such as bacte-ria, the genetic material consists merely of strands of DNA within the cell, generally loosely attached to the cell wall.

paralogous genes. Genes with highly similar function to other genes.

phenotype. The outward manifestation of the genotype*.

pleiotropy. The expression of a gene in more than one organ system. For instance, the genetic disease tuberous sclerosis is most often identified by the fatty tumors present on the skin. However, the same gene, which results in the production of a fatty material that the body can't use, also affects the brain and heart of many victims of the condition.

point mutation. A mutation* that can be assigned to a single site on a chro-mosome*. The usual result, if there is any, is the substitution of a single amino acid in a protein* molecule.

polyploid. Having more than one pair of chromosome* sets.

principle of parsimony. Sometimes called "Occam's razor." The logical principle that the simplest explanation that fits all of the actual data is the best.

proteins. Complex combinations of amino acids* that are the basic component of living cells.

races. Population groups that differ in the frequency of certain genes in their gene pools.

recessive gene. A gene that does not show up, except perhaps in a minimal fashion, in a heterozygote (see heterozygous*), but which is expressed in a homozygote (see homozygous*).

regulatory gene. A gene that controls the expression of another gene. The control could be of an on-off nature. For instance, it could control the time of onset and end of some growth pattern.

Renpenning's syndrome. An eponym for non-specific X-linked mental subnormality*.

right brain. A term frequently applied to half of the cerebral cortex, usually on the same side of the body as the dominant hand, whence the name. In it are located centers for the production of speech, and probably for spatial perception, higher mathematical reasoning, and other specialized abilities.

RNA. A genetic coding material, very similar to DNA*, which has special functions in the genetic functions of higher organisms, and which is the sole genetic material is some very simple life forms such as viruses.

selection (evolutionary). A shorthand term for the evolutionary process by which certain genotypes* survive and reproduce at a greater rate than others. Darwin specified two types of such selection, natural and sexual.

sex chromosomes. The chromosomes* that determine the sex of a higher organism. In humans and higher animals, two X-chromosomes normally produce a female; an X-chromosome* and a Y-chromosome*, a male.

sex linked. Controlled by genes on a sex (X or Y) chromosome*.

sexual selection. The process by which certain genotypes* increase in relative numbers in succeeding generations because they result in phenotypes* with a higher reproductive rate and possibly a shorter generation interval.

spatial perception. The ability to perceive spatial relationships. It is a primary factor in mechanical ability and possibly in graphic art.

Stanford-Binet Intelligence Test. A revised and refined version of the original Binet test, frequently used for diagnosis of mental subnormality* and for general intellectual assessment.

structural gene. A gene coding for the sequence of amino acids* in a protein*.

subspecies. Variants within a species. Subspecies can interbreed successfully with others of the same species. Thus, under the "Adam" theory, *Homo erectus** and *Homo sapiens** were subspecies rather than separate species.

theory. An analysis of the relationship of facts to one another. Under strict scientific interpretation, a theory cannot be proven, although hypotheses* based on a theory may be.

translocation. The exchange of parts within a chromosome* or a set of chromosomes.

variance. In statistics, the square of the standard deviation, used as a measure of the variability of a characteristic in samples or populations.

Wechsler Adult Intelligence Scale (WAIS). A standardized test widely used for the intellectual evaluation of persons over the age of 16 years. The test has two halves, verbal and performance, each of which provides a separate IQ score in addition to the full-scale IQ.

Wechsler Intelligence Scale for Children (WISC). A standardized test used for the evaluation of children between the ages of 6 and 16. The test, like the WAIS, has two halves and yields separate verbal and performance IQs as well as a full-scale IQ.

X-chromosome. One of the two types of sex chromosomes*, as opposed to autosomes*. A person (or other higher animal) having two X-chromosomes is normally female. When the complement is an X-chromosome

plus a Y-chromosome, the individual is a male. In addition to its function in sex determination, the X-chromosome has other genes affecting,
directly or indirectly, every body system.

X-linked. Controlled or mediated by genes on the X-chromosome*.

X-linked mental subnormality. Mental subnormality* resulting from defective genes on the X-chromosome*. In some cases the X-linked genes
lead to physiological disorders that affect the functioning of the brain.
Examples are Hurler's syndrome, Lesch-Nyhan syndrome, and the Edwards type of hydrocephalus. In other cases (those discussed in this
book) the condition is non-specific. That is, it has no readily discernable
symptoms other than lowered intelligence. However, the fragile-X condition (see fragile-X syndrome*) and macro-orchidism may be *secondary*
symptoms of nonspecific X-linked mental subnormality. (See also non-
specific X-linked mental subnormality*.)

Y-chromosome. The other sex chromosome. Persons and higher animals
with a Y-chromosome in addition to an X-chromosome* are normally
phenotypic (see phenotype*) males. While the X-chromosome carries
many identifiable genes other than those for sex determination, the Y-
chromosome does not. Its function seems to be almost entirely the production of maleness and the remedying of the individual for the lack of
a second X-chromosome.

Y-linkage. Control or mediation by genes on the Y-chromosome*.

References

Adler, T. (1995). Lineage of Y chromosome boosts Eve theory. *Science News, 147,* 326.

Allen, W., Herndon, C. N. & Dudley, F. C. (1944). Some examples of the inheritance of mental deficiency: Apparently sex-linked idiocy microcephaly. *American Journal of Mental Deficiency, 48,* 325-334.

American College of Medical Genetics. (1996). Policy statement. Bethesda, MD: *Xfraxa* (Internet http://www.worx.net/fraxa).

Anastasi, A. (1958). *Differential psychology.* (3rd. ed). New York: Macmillan.

Anastasi, A. (1972). Four hypotheses with a dearth of data: Response to Lehrke's "A theory of X-linkage of major intellectual traits." *American Journal of Mental Deficiency, 76,* 620-622.

Andreasen, N. C., Flaum, M., Swayze, V., O'Leary, D. S., Alliger, R., Cohen, G., Ehrhardt, J., & Yuh, W. T. C. (1993). Intelligence and brain structure in normal individuals. *American Journal of Psychiatry, 1516,* 130-134.

Associated Press. (1986, Mar. 25). We're all from 'African Eve'? *San Diego Union,* A3.

Associated Press. (1989, Jan. 16). Human language origins may lie in African genes, says biochemist. *San Diego Union,* A3.

Ayala, F. J. (Ed).. (1976). *Molecular evolution.* Sunderland, MA: Sinauer.

Baker, J. R. (1981). *Race.* Athens, GA: Foundation for Human Understanding.

Baumeister, A. A. (1967). Learning abilities of the mentally retarded. In A. A. Baumeister, (Ed.) *Mental retardation: Appraisal, education, and rehabilitation,* 181-209. Chicago: Aldine Publishing Co.

Bayley, N. (1966). Developmental problems of the mentally retarded child. In I. Phillips, (Ed.), *Prevention and treatment of mental retardation,* 85-110. New York: Basic Books.

Bearn, A. G. & Parker, W. C. (1965). *Genetics and evolution in three human serum proteins.* White Plains, NY: National Foundation-March of Dimes Birth Defects Foundation Original Article No. OAS-17.

Begley, S. & Carey, J. (1984, Apr. 3). Man's family portrait. *Newsweek.*

Begley, S. (1992, Mar. 2). Eve takes another fall. *Newsweek.*

Bell, E. T. (1937). *Men of mathematics.* New York: Simon and Schuster.

Benbow, C. P. & Stanley, J. C. (1980). Sex differences in mathematical ability: Fact or artifact? *Science, 210,* 1262-1264.

Benbow, C. P. & Stanley, J. C. (1981). Mathematical ability: Is sex a factor? *Science, 212,* 118-119.

Benbow, C. P. & Stanley, J. C. (1983). Sex differences in mathematical reasoning ability: More facts. *Science, 222,* 1029-1031.

Berg, E. (1966). Andssvage problemets omfang i Danmark. *Socialt Tidsskrift (Koben-haun), 5-6,* 150-162.

Bishop, J. E. (1991, Dec. 12) New gene test reliably detects retardation. *The Wall Street Journal,* B1, B5.

Bock, R. D. & Kolakowski, D. (1973). Further evidence of sex-linked major-gene influence on human spatial visualizing ability. *American Journal of Human Genetics, 25,* 1-14.

Bower, B. (1989, July 8). The talk of ages. *Science News, 136,* 24-26.

Bower, B. (1996a, July 13). Rational mind designs. *Science News, 150,* 24-25.

Bower, B. (1996b, Sept. 28). Human origins recede in Australia. *Science News, 150,* 196.

British Columbia Department of Health Services and Hospital Insurance. (1971). *Registry for handicapped children and adults: Annual report, 1970.* Vancouver: British Columbia Dept. of Health Services.

British Columbia Department of Health Services and Hospital Insurance. (1972). *Registry for handicapped children and adults: Annual report, 1971.* Vancouver: British Columbia Dept. of Health Services.

Brown, M. H. (1990). *The Search for Eve.* New York: Harper and Row.

Burnham, S. (1993). *America's bimodal crisis: Black intelligence in white society.* (2nd ed.) Athens, GA: Foundation for Human Understanding.

Busing backfires (Editorial). (1978, Sept. 18). Duluth, MN. Duluth Tribune.

Cann, R. L., Stoneking, M. & Wilson, A. C. (1987). Mitochondrial DNA and human evolution. *Nature, 325,* 31-36.

Coleman, J. S. (1966). *Equality of educational opportunity.* Washington: U.S. Dept. of Health, Education and Welfare.

Coon, C. S. (1962a). *The story of Man.* (2nd. ed.) New York: Knopf.

Coon, C. S. (1962b). *The origin of races.* New York: Knopf.

Coon, C. S. (1982). *Racial adaptations.* Chicago: Nelson-Hall.

Darwin, C. (1871). *The descent of Man and selection in relation to sex.* New York: The Modern Library.

de la Cruz, F. F. (1985). Fragile-X syndrome. *American Journal of Mental Deficiency, 90,* 119-123.

Dobzhansky, T. (1962). *Mankind evolving.* New Haven: Yale University Press.

Dobzhansky, T. (1970). *Genetics of the evolutionary process.* New York: Columbia University Press.

Dunn, H. G., Renpenning, H., Gerrard, J. W., Miller, J. R., Tabata, T. & Federoff, S. (1963). Mental retardation as a sex-linked defect. *American Journal of Mental Deficiency, 67,* 827-848.

Durant, W. (1943). *The story of philosophy*. Garden City, NY: Garden City Publishing.

Edey, M. A. & Johanson, D. C. (1989). *Blueprints: Solving the Mystery of Evolution*. Boston: Little Brown and Co.

Educational Testing Service (1994). *Sex, race, ethnicity, and performance on the GRE® General Test*. Publication No. 250347. Princeton, NJ: Graduate Record Examination Board.

Ellis, H. (1904). *Man and woman: A study of human secondary sexual characteristics*. (4th ed.) London: Walter Scott Publishing Co.

Eysenck, H. J. & Kamin, L. (1981). *The intelligence controversy*. New York: John Wiley and Sons.

Frazetta, T. H. (1975). *Complex adaptations in evolving populations*. Sunderland, MA: Sinauer.

Gilder, G. (1995, Feb. 26). Second thoughts on IQ, race, and poverty. San Diego: *The San Diego Union-Tribune*, G-4.

Goodenough, U. (1978). *Genetics* (2nd ed.). New York: Holt, Rinehart and Winston.

Graham, R. K. (1989). Five changepoints of intelligence. *The Mankind Quarterly, XXIX*, 129-141.

Gruenberg, E. M. (1964). Epidemiology. In H. A. Stevens & R. Heber (Eds.). *Mental retardation*, 259-306. Chicago: University of Chicago Press.

Hasan, K. Z. (1972). Mental retardation in Pakistan. In D. A. A. Primrose (Ed.), *Proceedings of the Second Congress of the International Association for the Scientific Study of Mental Retardation*, 61-73. Warsaw, Poland: Polish Medical Publishers.

Hedges, S. B., Kumar, S., Tamura, K. and Stoneking, M. (1992) Untitled Technical Comment. *Science*, 737-739.

Herrnstein, R. J. & Murray, C. (1994). *The bell curve*. New York: The Free Press.

Imre, P. D. (1968). The epidemiology of mental retardation in a S. E. rural USA community. In B. W. Richards (Ed.), *Proceedings of the First Congress of the International Association for the Scientific Study of Mental Deficiency* 550-565. Reigate (Surrey), Great Britain: Michael Jackson Publ.

Ingle, D. J. (1968). The need to investigate average biological differences among racial groups. In M. Mead, T. Dobzhansky, E. Tobach & R. E. Light, (Eds.) *Science and the concept of race*. New York: Columbia University Press.

Itzkoff, S. W. (1992). *The road to equality: Evolution and social reality*. Westport, CT: Praeger.

Itzkoff, S. W. (1994). *The decline of intelligence in America*. Westport, CT: Praeger.

Jensen, A. R. (1969a). *Environment, heredity and intelligence*. Cambridge, MA: Harvard Educational Review.

Jensen, A. R. (1969b). How much can we boost IQ and scholastic achievement? *Harvard Educational Review, 39*, 1-123.

Jensen, A. R. (1971). The race x sex x ability interaction. In R. Cancro (Ed.). *Intelligence: Genetic and environmental influences* 107-161. New York: Grune and Stratton.

Jensen, A. R. (1971, Sept. 9). Lecture before the Fourth International Congress of Human Genetics. Paris, France.

Jensen, A. R. (1974). How biased are culture-loaded tests? *Genetic Psychology Monographs, 90*, 185-244.

Johanson, D. & Johanson, L. (1994). *Ancestors: In search of human origins*. New York: Villard Books.

Johnson, G. E. (1897). Contribution to the psychology and pedagogy of feeble-minded children. *Journal of Psycho-Asthenics, 2*, 26-32.

Kurtén, B. (1972). *Not from the apes*. New York: Vantage Books.

Kuttner, R. E. (1968). Letters to and from the editor. *Perspect. Biol. Medicine, 11*, 707-709.

Lafee, S. (1995, Dec. 27). The brain gain. *The San Diego Union-Tribune,* E-1,4.

Lehrke, R. G. (1968). *Sex-linked mental retardation and verbal disability*. Ph.D. dissertation, University of Wisconsin, Madison, WI: Ann Arbor, MI: University Microfilms.

Lehrke, R. G. (1972a). A theory of X-linkage of major intellectual traits. *American Journal of Mental Deficiency, 76*, 611-619.

Lehrke, R. G. (1972b). Response to Dr. Anastasi and to the Drs. Nance and Engel. *American Journal of Mental Deficiency, 76*, 626-631.

Lehrke, R. G. (1974). *X-linked mental retardation and verbal disability*. In the National Foundation - March of Dimes, Birth Defects Original Article Series, Vol. 10, No. 1. Miami, FL: Symposia Specialists.

Lehrke, R. G. (1978). Sex linkage: A biological basis for greater male variability in intelligence. In R. T. Osborne, C. E. Noble, & N. Weyl (Eds.) *Human variation: The biopsychology of age, race and sex*. San Diego: Academic Press.

Lewandowski, R. C. Jr., Yunis, J. J., Lehrke, R., O'Leary, J., Swaiman, K. F., & Sanchez, O. (1976). Trisomy for the distal half of the short arm of chromosome 9. *American Journal of Diseases of Children, 130*, 663-667.

Losowsky, M. S. (1961). Hereditary mental defect showing the pattern of sex influence. *Journal of Mental Deficiency Research, 5*, 60-62.

Lubs, H. A. (1969). A marker-X chromosome. *American Journal of Human genetics, 21*, 244.

Lynn, R. (1991). Race differences in intelligence: A global perspective. *Mankind Quarterly, XXXI*, 255-296.

Lyon, M. P. (1962). Sex chromatin and gene action in the mammalian X-chromo some. *American Journal of Human Genetics, 14*, 135-148.

Martin, J. P. and Bell, J. (1943). A pedigree of mental defect showing sex linkage. *Journal of Neurological Psychiatry, N. S. 6*, 154-157.

Mayr, E. (1970). *Population, species, and evolution*. Cambridge, MA: Harvard University Press.

McKusick, V. A. (1964). *On the X-chromosome of Man*. Washington: American Institute of Biological Sciences.

Montagu, A. (1962). *Culture and the evolution of Man*. New York: Oxford University Press.

Montagu, A. (1969). *Man: His first two million years*. New York: Columbia University Press.

Morris, D. (1967). *The naked ape*. New York: McGraw-Hill.

Nance, W. E. & Engel, E. (1972) One X and four hypotheses: Response to Lehrke's "A theory of X-linkage of major intellectual traits". *American Journal of Mental Deficiency, 76*, 623-625.

Neel, J. V. (1970). Lessons from a "primitive" people. *Science, 170*, 815-822.

Neel, J. V., Salzano, F. M., Junqueira, P. C., Kreiter, F, & Maybury-Lewis, D. (1964). Studies on the Xavante Indians of the Brazilian Mato Graso. *Human Genetics, 16*, 52-140.

New York State Department of Mental Hygiene, Mental Health Research Unit. (1955). *Technical report: A special census of suspected referred mental retardation, Onondaga County, N.Y.* Syracuse, NY: Syracuse University Press.

Opitz, J. M. and Sutherland, G. R. (1984). Conference report on the Fragile X and X-linked mental retardation. *American Journal of Medical Genetics, 17*, 5-94.

Opitz, J. M. (1986). Editorial comment: On the gates of hell and a most unusual gene. In J. M. Opitz (Ed.) *X-linked mental retardation 2.* (Special edition of the *American Journal of Medical Genetics, 23*, 1-10).

Outhit, M. C. (1933). A study of the resemblance of parents and children in general intelligence. *Archives of Psychology, 149*, 1-60.

Pauling, L. (1963). Molecular disease and evolution. *Bulletin of the New York Academy of Medicine, 40*, No. 5.

Penrose, L.S. (1963). *The biology of mental defect.* New York: Grune and Stratton.

Perlman, D. (1995, May 2). Sophisticated tools came out of Africa. *The San Diego Union Tribune,* E-5.

Pfeiffer, J. E. (1972). *The emergence of Man,* (2nd ed.). New York: Harper and Row.

Pilbeam, D. (1970). *The evolution of Man.* New York: Funk and Wagnalls.

Planck, M. (1949). *Scientific autobiography and other papers.* Westport, CT: Greenwood Press.

Reed, E. W. & Reed, S. C. (1965). *Mental retardation: A family study.* Philadelphia: Saunders.

Reed, T. E. (1969). Caucasian genes in American negroes. *Science, 165*, 762-768.

Renpenning, H., Gerrard, J. W., Zaleski, W. A. & Tabata, T. (1962). Familial sex-linked mental retardation. *Canadian Medical Association Journal, 87*, 954-956.

Reschly, D. J. & Ward, S. M. (1991). Use of adaptive behavior measures and over-representation of black students in programs for students with mild mental retardation. *American Journal on Mental Retardation, 96*, 257-268.

Richardson, W. P. & Higgins, A. C. (1964). A survey of handicapping conditions and handicapped children in Alamance County, North Carolina. *American Journal of Public Health, 54*, 1817-1830.

Roberts, J. A. F., Norman, R. M. & Griffiths, R. (1945). On the difference between the sexes in the dispersion of intelligence. *British Medical Journal, 1*, 727-730.

Ross, C. A. & Folstein, S. E. (1993 Summer). New directions in HD research. *The Marker* (Huntington's Disease Society of America), 6, 5.

Ruvalcaba, R. H. A., Mhyre, S.A., Roosen-Runge, E. C. & Beckwith, J. B. (1977). X-linked mental deficiency megalotestes syndrome. *Journal of the American Medical Assn., 238*, 1646-1650.

Scottish Council for Research in Education. (1949). *The trend of Scottish intelligence.* London: University of London Press.

Seligman, D. (1992). *A question of intelligence.* New York: Birch Lane.

Socialstyrelsen. (1972, May 15). *Living standards in Swedish facilities for the mentally retarded.* Special report. Stockholm: Socialstyrelsen.

Sowell, T. (1993). *Inside American Education.* New York: The Free Press.

Stafford, R. E. (1961). Sex differences in spatial visualization as evidence of sex-linked inheritance. *British Medical Journal, 13*, 727-730.

Stapleton, S. H. (1978, Sept.). Where school promotions have to be earned. *Reader's Digest*, 65-74.

Sterner, R. (1967). *Note on the number of retarded children in Vasternorrland County, Sweden.* Paper presented at the International League of Societies for the Mentally Handicapped, Stockholm, Sweden.

Stevens, W. K. (1992, Feb. 18). Neanderthals' link to man is debated. *New York Times News Service in The San Diego Union-Tribune*, C3.

Stomma, D. & Wald, I. (1972). *The influence of medical rehabilitation on the general performance of institutionalized mentally retarded children.* Warsaw, Poland: Psychoneurological Institute.

Swartz, M. J. & Jordan, D. K. (1976). *Anthropology: Perspective on Humanity.* New York: John Wiley and Sons, Inc.

Templeton, A. R. (1992, Feb. 7). Human origins and analysis of mitochondrial DNA sequences (technical comment). *Science, 737.*

Terman, L. M. (1925). *Genetic studies of genius, Vol. 1.* Stanford, CA: Stanford Univ. Press.

Travis, J. (1995). When CAG spells trouble. DNA repeats may turn good proteins bad. *Science News, 147*, 360-361.

Turner, G. & Turner, B. (1974). X-linked mental retardation. *Journal of Medical Genetics, 11*, 109-113.

Turner, G. (1996). Intelligence and the X-chromosome. *Lancet, 347,* 1814-1815.

U.S. Bureau of the Census. (1989). *Statistical abstract of the United States: 1989,* (109th ed.). Washington, DC: U.S. Government Printing Office.

U.S. Bureau of the Census. (1990). *Statistical abstract of the United States: 1990,* (110th edition). Washington, DC: U.S. Government Printing Office.

Van Court, M. & Bean, F. D. (1985). Intelligence and fertility in the U.S.: 1912-1982. *Intelligence, 9*, 23-32.

Vandenberg, S. G. (1962). The hereditary abilities study: Hereditary components in a psychological test battery. *American Journal of Human Genetics, 14*, 220-237.

Verbraak, P. (1975). A new prevalence figure for mental retardation in the Netherlands. In D. A. A. Primrose (Ed.), *Proceedings of the Third Congress of the International Association for the Scientific Study of Mental Retardation,* 664-673. Warsaw: Polish Medical Publishers.

Vigilante, L., Stoneking, M., Harpending, H., Hawkes, K. & Wilson, A. C. (1991). African populations and the evolution of human mitochondrial DNA. *Science, 253*, 1503-1507.

Volpe, E. P. (1981). *Understanding evolution,* (4th ed.). Dubuque, IA: Wm. C. Brown.

Wechsler, D. (1958). *The measurement of adult intelligence.* (4th ed.) Baltimore: Williams and Wilkins.

Weidenreich, F. (1946). *Apes, Giants, and Man.* Chicago: University of Chicago Press.

Weiss, M. L. & Mann, A. E. (1985) *Human Biology and Behavior (4th ed.)* Boston: Little, Brown & Co.

Weiss, V. (1991). It could be neo-Lysenkoism, if there was ever a break in continuity. *Mankind Quarterly, XXXI*, 231-253.

Wunsch, W. L. (1951). The first complete tabulation of the Rhode Island Mental Deficiency Record. *American Journal of Mental Deficiency, 55,* 293-312.

Young, P. (1989). Cutting away the DNA the mitochondrial way. *Science News, 136,* 6, 85.

Index